FOUR NOTABLE SCOTS

House of the Earl of Stirling, known as the Argyle Lodging.

FOUR NOTABLE SCOTS

BY

T. CROUTHER GORDON
D.F.C., B.D., Ph.D.

FOREWORD BY

EMERITUS PROFESSOR JOHN D. MACKIE,
C.B.E., M.C., M.A., LL.D.

Historiographer Royal in Scotland

ENEAS MACKAY
STIRLING

First Published - *1960*

Printed at
The Observer Press, Stirling, Scotland

CONTENTS

5

ILLUSTRATIONS

FOREWORD

In these wholesale days when everything is being measured by the same rod, it is pleasant to have a reminder of the truth that a country, even a small country like Scotland, is a unity composed of many variant parts, and that each component locality has a history and a character of its own.

Dr. Crouther Gordon, who has already commended himself to a wide public by his admirable book on David Allan, the son of the Shoremaster of Alloa, now adds to our gratitude by a further work of piety towards the countryside in which he dwells.

He presents to us the lives of four distinguished sons of Clackmannanshire whose careers, though they added distinction to the place of their origin, influenced the history not only of Scotland but of the British Empire and in some sense of the whole world.

William Alexander, the " guidman of Menstrie," who became the first Earl of Stirling, was a kenspeckle figure in his day, in his manysidedness not unworthy of comparison with Sir Walter Raleigh. If he is to be censured for his monopoly of some of the coinage in Scotland, it must be remembered that Raleigh had monopolies for tin, cards and sweet wine. The granting of a monopoly was a way of rewarding public service in those days and it was sometimes defended as being in the public interest. Whether Alexander's experiments with the currency benefited the country may be doubted, but they conferred no great advantage upon the experimenter, who died bankrupt in the end. His poetry was more admired in his own day than it is now, and some of his work as Secretary was unpopular with his fellow Scots; but a man must be judged by the standards of his time and Alexander, by whatever standards he is judged, must be applauded as one who had a living vision of a great Scotland overseas.

" Bobbing John " of the '15 has usually appeared in history as the uncertain politician of the reign of Queen Anne and the hesitant general of Sheriffmuir. Yet he had his qualities, as Dr. Crouther Gordon shows; and if he made mistakes he paid for them.

Sir Ralph Abercromby, on the other hand, is a figure who has always commanded admiration and who has deserved it. It was he and his fellow Scot, Sir John Moore, who were the real creators of " that astonishing infantry" which was to shatter the hopes of Napoleon, and the secret of their achievement was their concern for the private soldier.

The last of the heroes, Sir James Wylie, is less well-known than he deserves to be. He was one of that great band of Scotsmen who set their mark upon the history of Russia. Samuel Greig, the son of a shipmaster at Inverkeithing, the real maker of the Russian navy; Barclay de Tolly, a scion of the house of Towie in Aberdeenshire, who played so great a part in defeating Napoleon; Charles Cameron, the architect of so many fine buildings; doctors like Erskine, the physician of Peter the Great, and Garven, who even penetrated to China;—all these were great figures in their day. Beside them James Wylie from Kincardine-on-Forth deserves to take his place. His story is admirably told by Dr. Crouther Gordon, to whom we are particularly grateful for the account of Betty Wilcox who sought (and won) the Czar's favour by knitting him a pair of socks.

All lovers of the shire of Clackmannan, and all lovers of Scotland, will be glad to be reminded of the great men who had their origin in the pleasant land which lies to the north of the Forth between Stirlingshire and the Kingdom of Fife. For that land I have an affection. Some of my own forebears came from Kincardine, which, when first I knew it, then still belonged, I think, to the county of Perthshire. Then the town still welcomed to its little pier not only the steamers which plied regularly between Leith and Stirling, but the ships which brought esparto grass for the paper mills. It is pleasant to think that though the appearance of the Forth Bridge has to some extent altered the condition of that gracious countryside, much of the old grace, and, as this book shows, much of the old spirit, survives intact.

J. D. MACKIE.

PREFACE

THE historian's task is never done for he must interpret the past to each new age. The men who shaped the past and consequently the present call continually for re-assessment, and if, even in the light of research, the verdict has to be the same as before, it is enough reward for the writer to remind the men of to-day of their notable ancestors.

These historical sketches of Scotsmen of the past are presented to show that in the centre of Scotland in the seventeenth and eighteenth centuries certain figures exerted a remarkable influence on the fortunes of our nation. Within the short stretch of territory from Stirling to Dunfermline, comprising roughly the area of Clackmannanshire, distinguished statesmen and soldiers arose, who through their personal qualities decided the kind of people we were to become.

Nor was their influence confined to Scotland. In the case of Sir William Alexander, his bold dream of a new empire in America, visualised as Nova Scotia, gave the start to what is to-day the mighty, developing Dominion of Canada, and in the case of Sir James Wylie, his personal predominance over the minds and policies of successive Czars had a real effect on the Napoleonic Wars. The victory of Sir Ralph Abercromby at Aboukir, too, was if anything more decisive for the history of the world than the parallel triumph of Montgomery at El Alamein. As for the sixth Earl of Mar, his work in framing the Union of the Kingdoms in 1707 turned a new page in the prosperity of the Island, and though less spectacular was much more enduring than his romantic Rising. Altogether it is an interesting quartet of Scotsmen.

In the case of each of these Scots, I have had to take into account the contentions of their enemies, for all of them were subjected to campaigns of vituperation and malice. No man can make an impact on his age without evoking from some quarter an unfavourable reaction. It has been a delicate point to decide in these circumstances where facts cease and prejudice begins. On the whole I have tried to bring out the better qualities of the man, for I freely allow that even in the finest characters there are to be found weaknesses and faults. My aim, however, has been rather to assess the total achievement of each Scot and to deny no credit where credit is due. The total impression is, I venture to think, somewhat heartening for those who would think well of the human race and especially that part of it in Scotland.

My hope is that younger Scots will read these sketches with some interest and not a little pride, and that older ones will see more clearly the unique contributions of these four notables to the life of our people.

Since these pages are not so much for the pundit and scholar as for the average, interested and seeking reader, they are not burdened with footnotes or references. The expert will know where the facts come from, and the others will not worry.

It is a good augury for the Scotland of to-day that the Scotland of yesterday produced four such outstanding leaders.

The proofs have been corrected by Dr. William R. Aitken, M.A., F.R.S.A., F.L.A., the Librarian of the County of Ayr, and for this and many other kindnesses he deserves my gratitude.

Thanks for the use of illustrations are due to the Rt. Hon. The Earl of Mar and Kellie ; the Director of the Scottish National Portrait Gallery ; Messrs. T. & R. Annan & Sons ; and Mr. Henry Murray.

Mr. Walter McK. Murray, A.L.A., the County Librarian of Clackmannan, and his staff, are due a special word of thanks for unfailing courtesy and help, especially in securing rare volumes.

T. CROUTHER GORDON.

CHAPTER I

THE VERSATILE EARL OF STIRLING

Poet - Courtier - Coloniser

MENSTRIE CASTLE lies snugly at the foot of the Ochil Hills, sheltered on the north by the grassy slopes that rise up to Dumyat and commanding on the south a broad sweeping view of level country to the winding links of Forth and beyond. Down the wooded glen come tumbling the splashing waters that for many a year turned the wheels of the mill and supplied the needs of the quiet village. As it stands to-day, still occupied but semi-ruined, it smacks something of its old grandeur and flaunts its solitary turret in the air.

In this typical Scots manor house two Scots of eminence were born. One was Sir Ralph Abercromby, who died in the hour of victory at Aboukir, thwarting, like General Montgomery, the plans of a European dictator. The other was William Alexander, two centuries before him, who, beginning simply as " the guidman of Menstrie," rose by sheer ability and shrewd courtiership to become the Secretary of State for Scotland and the first Earl of Stirling. But these two Scots were alike only in their birthplace and their title ; in all other points they were diverse. The first died with the gratitude of a whole nation for breaking Napoleon's threat to Egypt ; the second died a hopeless and hated bankrupt.

And yet William Alexander was a versatile and fascinating man. It is claimed that he was an even more representative character of his age than Sir Walter Raleigh, and it was a great age of Renaissance genius. Certain it is that he was far and away the most powerful personality in Scotland in the first quarter of the seventeenth century. Little happened in the political world but Alexander sanctioned if not engineered it. The signature might be that of James: but the pen was the pen of Stirling. His interests ranged from founding Nova Scotia to minting a new coinage, from silver-mining to sonnets, and nothing was alien to his Renaissance mind. With all his faults, Alexander still grips us with a perennial fascination.

The Alexanders had been in Menstrie for many a day. Men of substance all, one of them in 1506 was appointed an arbiter in a dispute on boundaries between the Abbot of Cambuskenneth and Bruce of Clackmannan. Like many other small, landed gentry, the Alexanders claimed descent from Somerled, Lord of the Isles. They boasted of links with Robert II and Robert III. Indeed, so keen was William Alexander himself to establish his lineage that he induced Archibald Alexander of Tarbert in 1631 to come and live with him at Menstrie and while there to accept him as chief of the clan. Apart from this, the Alexanders preserved contacts with the great family of the Argyles, and through this they secured charters of the lands and barony of Menstrie.

William's own father died on the 10th of February, 1581, leaving him as a lad of four to face the topsy-turvy Scotland of his day. McGrail, the latest biographer, seems to be right in placing his birth in 1577. Little wonder, then, that his uncle, James Alexander, a burgess of Stirling, was made the boy's guardian. The future Secretary of State was a keen scholar, well-grounded in the Classics by Thomas, the equally competent brother of George Buchanan. Of all the better class of that day in Scotland, the young laird of Menstrie had the firmest

grasp of classical lore and history. The range of knowledge revealed by the Four Monarchick Tragedies is
truly encyclopædic. This could scarcely have been all
acquired at a school in Stirling. Which university did
the budding scholar attend? David Laing concluded
it was St. Andrews; McUre in 1775 suggested it was
Glasgow and McGrail gives grounds for confirming this.
There was, at any rate, a soft spot in his heart for Glasgow,
and all his sons whose education we can trace attended
the classes in Glasgow University. He later secured
bursaries for scholars there and gifted £500 Scots for
rooms near the college.

Drummond of Hawthornden, who was on the closest
terms of intimacy with Alexander, asserts that the young
Menstrie laird got " his breeding at Leiden," and though
the register at the Dutch university does not contain his
name, he could well have studied as an irregular student.

But even more valuable as education than Leiden
was Alexander's travel on the Continent. Castle Campbell
was within an easy ride from Menstrie and his wide cultural
interests soon introduced young Alexander there. The
youthful Earl of Argyle, going on an extended tour,
took this erudite scholar with him and together they saw
the Loire, the Po and the Apennines, rivers that were to
appear in the " Aurora " in 1604.

In 1597, perhaps as the fruit of their intimacy, Argyle
gave him by charter " the Five Pund land of Mains of
Menstrie," which in 1605 was increased to include the
whole of Menstrie. By 1607 he had secured also the
mineral rights of the land, and so William Alexander
was started on that strange career of acquisition and
money-getting that made him the wonder and the scorn
of his age.

That " the guidman of Menstrie " was ambitious

no one can deny : that he was avaricious is a libel. Starting with little, he engaged in the fight for glittering prizes, knowing full well that prestige and money were essential to win them. The influence came early, for Argyle soon introduced him to James VI and speedily he was on terms of literary intimacy with the king. Here was a cultural asset for the royal circle ; here was a poet who could cap each royal verse with another equally witty. For hours they sat together in purely literary pursuits. Although the political climber made many bitter enemies on his perilous ascent to power, it is worth noting that he retained to the end the confidence of James. Indeed, Charles Rogers goes further and claims that he " retained an ascendancy over the vacillating humours of the pedantic monarch." The king dubbed him, " my philosophical poet," and the published letters and charters give the clear impression that the monarch danced to each tune that the subject played. It is an incredible record of royal pliancy, for the exploiter and coloniser had only to whisper his newest plan and the signature of James gave it full authority. Alexander was, without doubt, a very cunning fellow.

Royal favour came early. The black night of poetical darkness in Scotland was lit up in 1603 by the appearance of a long, ambitious, dramatic poem about Darius, and readers found that it had been dedicated to no less a patron than the King himself. And James was pleased ! Scots poets were indeed scarce and here was one moulded on the grand scale. At once the royal patron chained such genius to his throne. Soon he made him tutor and companion to his heir, Prince Henry, and Alexander felt himself so quickly and so surely in the royal good graces that within a year he wrote for the youth a " Paranaesis," which warned the heir, among other things, that " wicked

THE CASTLE OF MENSTRIE.

princes may be dethroned." By 1607 he had started
that amazing list of royal bounties, which staggers a
modern mind. Through his marriage with the daughter
of Erskine of Balgonie, he secured a royal pension of £100
a year.

No figure in political history has been so fertile as
Alexander in extracting wealth from fallow fields. James
and he together devised scheme after scheme for extracting
monies. They discovered, for instance, that from 1547
to 1588 the Crown had lost arrears of taxes in Scotland.
Why not recover these, before it was too late? Let
Alexander make the attempt, and the king would allow
him a share of the spoil—up to a cool six thousand! Talk
about getting blood out of stone! True, the king got
his whack out of it, but as for the laird of Menstrie it
was a forlorn hope. Not a penny came to the optimistic
Scot! So, too, with the minerals of Menstrie. The
king got his royalties, but the laird whistled for his profits.
Was James such a fool after all?

By now the court had moved to London, and in his
court the king liked to have Alexander near him. It
reminded him of his happy days on the Ochils, hunting
with his falcons. He indicated his favour by making him
Sir William Alexander in 1608, which dignity the poet
could well sustain, for did not Sir James Shaw owe him
the goodly sum of seventeen thousand merks, and was
silver not coming from his Menstrie mine? It looks
like it, for in 1611 he was given the exclusive right to refine
silver for twenty-one years. It all looked so promising.
It was gambler's lure. He ventured further into silver-
mining. This time it was at Hilverston near Linlithgow,
and two others joined him in partnership. Since 1607
this mine had been worked for the king's own benefit,
but by 1613 James sold out to Alexander, who now sank

good money into a bad risk. By waning yield, by wilful damage and by deliberate theft, the hopeful venture turned out a financial disaster. By 1616 the dabbling laird was a poorer, a sadder, but, it is to be feared, not a wiser man.

For most of the year, now, Sir William was far away in London. The English nobility, with forgivable jealousy, could afford to scoff at some of the rude Scots that followed their monarch south to London, but the " philosophical poet " was in another category. He could stand their scrutiny. His encyclopædic knowledge rather frightened them, and his polished Elegy on the death of Prince Henry in 1612 proved that he could rise adequately to a great national occasion. As a " Gentleman of the Privy Chamber," he was on intimate terms with the Prince, who, according to John Buchan, had he been spared, would have avoided the pitfalls that brought Charles to the scaffold. This was a period of ample output from the poet's brain. In 1613 he carried through the ambitious and risky project of completing Sir Philip Sydney's unfinished "Arcadia." Anyone less modest would have shrunk from the very thought, but modesty never hindered Sir William. The achievement was no better and no worse than was to be expected.

But now his vastest poem was on the stocks. Through the sunny days of 1614, deep-embowered in his Menstrie Manor, he plunged into the apocalyptic terrors of his " Doomes-Day." True to the philosophical and religious thought of his day, he expresses the accepted picture of the world's judgment, and graphically traces the vast economy of Creation from the revolt of the Angels to the Great Day of the Lord. Through its eleven thousand, one hundred and twenty-eight lines he plunges on with dogged perseverance, lines that probably only the printer has ever read completely! Now and again, the theme itself imparts terror to the lines :—

"What agony doth thus my soul invest?
  I think I see heaven burn, hel's gulphs all gape,
  My panting heart doth beat upon my breast,
  As urging passage that it thence may scape . . ."

But no originality of thought marks the herculean effort. "Doomes-Day" remains a mighty monstrosity of poetry.

This was in some ways the happiest period of Sir William's whole life. Although in the thick of political life and intrigue, he drove north in the long, summer days and forgot high policies in the peace of his study at Menstrie. Nor was he alone. A couple of miles along the road, he could sharpen his wit on the profound and cultured mind of Alexander Hume of Logie, who, having discovered the emptiness of public political life, devoted his talents to the souls of a quiet parish. He was gone now, but his place was taken by Drummond of Hawthornden, than whom there was no finer spirit in Scotland. And now developed the tenderest literary friendship of seventeenth-century Scotland. It was the most selfless and beautiful thing in Alexander's life. It originated in 1606 when Drummond in reading the "Aurora" found for the first time a fellow-Scot who could rise lyrically on the wings of poesy, and he claimed then that the cold North had produced a poet, whose achievement was equal to the most heroic actions of the past. By 1612 he asserted that Alexander, by his "Elegy," had made "Doven" (Devon) Valley famous. In plain prose in 1614 he stated that Sir William was "that most excellent spirit and rarest gem of our North." What a charming picture that pen-artist draws of the rich, delightful life in Menstrie Castle! A warm welcome met him at the door, the children came prattling to his knee, so much so that he would fain have adopted one as his very own. The table groaned with good things, but even without such cheer, the occasion would have been happy in the company of " the guidman of Menstrie." After dining in Homeric fashion, the tables were cleared, the children banished and the lords of poesy settled down to high literary themes and projects. Drummond soon learned to value Alexander himself even more highly than his ambitious poems, and especially he prized the grace and courtesy of the man. Most unwillingly he tore himself away from the cosy fire and congenial company in Menstrie Castle. And the friendship lasted. Long after 1620 the mutual admiration continued, and amid the bitter political intrigues of the court, Alexander was comforted by the wise and sympathetic messages that flowed southwards from the quiet study at Hawthornden. " The greatest conquest that I have made on earth is that I am assured ye love my remembrance," said Drummond. In another letter he asserts that his best epitaph would be to be worthy of Alexander's friendship. He deplores that the court-poet in London has not " the Sovereignty of all Parnassus ; I had almost said the world save I fear to meet with Treason."

When Ben Jonson had his memorable talk at Hawthornden in 1618, the topics ranging from " Good Queen Bess " to Bacon, the poet of Menstrie also figured, and though Ben felt that Alexander—a power in the land—preferred Drayton to himself, yet Drummond upheld his brother-Scot, and ranked him above Donne and even on a par with Shakespeare. In the same year, 1618, he told Drayton himself that Alexander was " your matchless friend," while Drayton returned the compliment by calling the laird of Menstrie " that Man of Men," and the next year addresses him thus :—

" . . . and thou gentle Swayne
   That dost thy pipe by silver Doven sound,
   Alexis that dost with thy flocks remayne
   Far off within the Calydonian ground."

In 1627 he declares his love for " Menstry " even
more than for " his numbers, which were brave and hie."

Not only Drayton but also the gentle Samuel Daniel
remembered the Devon poet and wrote in his Epistle
of 1605 :—

" You have a Swannet of your own,
   Within the banks of Doven meditates
   Sweet notes to you, and unto your renowne
   The glory of his music dedicates."

Another lesser poet, the Aberdonian Arthur Johnston,
published his Epigrams in 1632, and in them so far forgot
himself as to compare the poet of Menstrie with Alexander
the Great. " Compare the Alexanders," he writes, " the
Macedonian was great by victorious arms, the Scot in
song. Which is greater ? "

It is scarcely credible to us to-day that the public,
poetical prestige of Alexander should have been so great
as to suggest the comparison. And yet Andrew Ramsay
in 1633 went even further by deeming the Scots poet more
powerful and compelling than the eloquent Demosthenes.
William Lithgow, the daring Scots traveller, is just as
fulsome in his praise, for in the year of Charles I's coronation, after acclaiming Nova Scotia, the child of
Alexander's brain, thus :—

" For which brave Menstrie, in his matchless merit
   Shall praise on earth, reward from Heaven merit,"

he goes on as follows :—

" So Menstrie, then, with Asia's great Commander,
   Shall twise succeed, a second Alexander."

To poets of a lesser calibre the great social and political prestige of Alexander no doubt appealed mightily, and one fears this distorted their judgment. Posterity, at any rate has not endorsed their verdict. Drummond, however, was not of that number, and perhaps he was thinking more of "Aurora" and the Sonnets, when he ranked his friend so high. As an index of the thought and rhetoric of his day even the Tragedies have their value.

But we must return to the actions of the statesmen and forget the creations of the poet. When James moved south in 1603 he was followed by hopeful place-mongers from the north, and for many a day the advice among the impecunious Scots was "haud sooth." The invasion became a plague to James, and he sought to apply the brake to it all. In 1619 he appointed Sir William to the unpopular task of prohibiting all persons passing from Scotland into England, unless they be gentlemen of good quality. Class legislation, with a vengeance! And yet it was not without good reason. As early as 1614 Menstrie had been made the Master of Requests for Scotland by royal letter, which makes it plain that worthless Scots were making themselves a nuisance to the king and shaming their native land. Alexander had the very distasteful task of packing these fellows north again or giving them licences to go abroad. As we shall see, both king and courtier came to realise that there were too many people living in Scotland for the land to support. It was time, so they put it, for the hive to swarm.

The post offered, clearly, unique chances for self-aggrandisement, for no approach of any kind could be made to the king without Alexander's written sanction, but it also made many gratuitous foes, and contributed to make him before he died the most detested man in the kingdom. And now, in 1619, to add to his unpopularity, he had to stop the train of place-seekers to the south.

Such a useful and important servant of His Majesty could hardly be kept from the inner council of the realm. It is not surprising that on the 1st of July, 1615, James promoted him to be a Privy Councillor, and within a fortnight in Edinburgh, with his hand on " The Holy Evangel," he swore allegiance to king and country. This brought the scholar-courtier into the mid-stream of politics, and he was soon to find there many conflicting cross-currents that opposed his progress. For one thing, he soon found that though the king might instruct the Council, the Council could be very procrastinating and very provocative. They were afraid of the Master of Requests, and were never sure whether the king was using the Secretary for some dark scheme of his own or the Secretary the king.

The summers of 1617/1620 were, we know, spent by Menstrie in his snug mansion at the Hillfoots, where he amused himself in his literary pursuits. Occasionally he was called to Edinburgh for meetings of the Privy Council, and in 1617 he personally accompanied James on his royal visit to Scotland. But he preferred to leave the cares of State and browse "in numbers" under the towering, grassy slopes of the Ochils. He worked doggedly at his " Doomes-Day," a theme that surely contrasted boldly with the peace and natural beauty of his country seat, and at this time he used his good offices to secure a useful legacy for the University of Glasgow, where his son at that time was a student. For many a day a monument in the Inner Quadrangle testified to the gratitude of the College, although, be it noted, it omits any mention of Alexander having been either a student or a graduate there.

It was in this quiet period—the last he was to enjoy—that " the guidman of Menstrie " conceived the vast and ambitious colonial scheme that was to prove both his glory and his shame. His claim upon posterity cannot be based on his vast output of poetry. He will, however, always deserve attention as the father of Nova Scotia, the visionary who saw clearly the emergence of a great empire beyond the sea. Perhaps he was prompted by the launching of the East India Company in 1600. Certainly he was not ignorant of the attempts by England to establish settlements in New England and Virginia. Nor with his ear so near the royal council-chamber could he forget the departure of the Pilgrim Fathers in 1620. His own testimony proves that he envied for Scotland the same privilege and promise that England enjoyed in the New World. By 1621 his colonial plan had taken shape. On the 5th of August, he asked the Privy Council to give a charter to Sir William Alexander under the Great Seal.

McGrail shows how Captain John Mason, governor of Newfoundland, had approached the Secretary, and fired his imagination with the possibilities of the new country. By the 29th of September, Menstrie had posted to Edinburgh and laid his hands on the charter. It is now a historic document, for it made him the Hereditary Lieutenant of a great tract of territory totalling 60,000 square miles from Cape Sable to the St. Croix River, which to-day is one of the richest and most prosperous parts of the globe. The amusing and most fantastic feature is that this was Nova Scotia, New Scotland, a virtual part of Old Scotland, a section of the Scottish kingdom.

The powers invested in the Lieutenant were breathtaking. These included rights to minerals, fisheries, taxes, sales of land, and exemption from all customs into Scotland for seven years and even the coining of

THE EARL OF STIRLING
(Scottish National Portrait Gallery).
By kind permission

money. As chief Justice and Admiral, he had the power of life and death, he could make and alter laws, and he could confer honours and grant charters of land on whom he would. A greater man might have been forgiven an intoxicating sense of power with such a charter, and yet Sir William was wise enough to know that the French Arcady was co-extensive with this very domain. He was to see a day when a new king would go back on his word, and the lieutenancy would hardly be worth the parchment and the seal.

Meanwhile he did not let the grass—even of Nova Scotia—grow under his feet. By November of the same year Robert Gordon had been made a knight and given the Cape Breton. A ship was equipped in London, and despatched to Kirkcudbright, where it was hoped through the family influence, some pioneers might be enlisted. But poverty and famine pre-occupied the natives, and only a blacksmith and a Presbyterian minister were brave enough to embark. After being held up at the Isle of Man, the ship finally made for the West, and failing to make Cape Breton owing to a gale, it had to winter in St. John's, Newfoundland. The blacksmith and the cleric being finally landed, did not survive the winter, for when the " St. Luke " arrived the following year, these two essential colonists were dead and the disorderly remnant of the crew had scattered.

The money for these expensive ventures came from the pocket of the Lieutenant of Nova Scotia, and it amounted to no less than £6,000 sterling. In vain did he try to extort this from the English Treasury. But he was not discouraged. On the contrary, the first rebuff but re-kindled his ardour. It certainly led him on directly to methods of money-raising that struck at the roots of the ancient aristocracy.

His first reaction—as one might expect—was a literary one. He took to paper and ink. When the news of the first failure reached him, he drew up with speed and yet not without grace of diction and glow his intriguing " Encouragement to Colonies." It is an appeal to Scotsmen to embark on the great enterprise of colonising Canada. If they treated it at that time with undeserved contempt and indifference, they have certainly since then redeemed their mistake, for have they not spread Scottish names across the Dominion from one side to the other ? If they have not succeeded, as was planned, in naming the St. Croix the River Tweed and the St. John the River Clyde, they have certainly placed Mackenzies and Frasers, Stewarts and Selkirks across the Continent. He called the land north of the Bay of Fundy Alexandria, and the estuary east of it he named the Firth of Forth. It was all neatly worked out on the map which was included in the book. But this flat map was dull, compared to the pen-pictures drawn by the versatile propagandist of Menstrie. It has been called " a masterpiece of impractical erudition . . . the work of a visionary idealist " (McGrail). Still, it was, within its limits, a thorough and enthusiastic effort to interest the more adventurous of his countrymen.

He began, in scholarly fashion, with the age of Shem, and swept the centuries with his pen to prove the reasonableness of colonising. Nova Scotia becomes, in his vivid imagination, a fair Elysium. In a passing reference to the French, he notes :—

> " Monsieur Champlain did cut a walk through the woods, where they delighted to repair in summer, to shroud themselves from the heat, and the rather that they had a sweet melody, which was made by the variety of voices of singing Birds, which without any affectation did afford them natural music."

Notice how Alexander pulls out every stop that can strike an answering chord in a Scottish heart. Now he rouses national feeling by claiming that if there is to be a New France and a New Spain, why should there not be a New Scotland?

> "I would rather betray the weakness of my power than conceal the greatness of my desire . . . that I shew them that my countrymen would never venture in such an enterprise unless it were as there were a New France and a New Spain and a New England, that they might likewise have a New Scotland . . ."

This was well-calculated to stir the sullen hearts of Old Scotia.

But if the powerful motive of jealousy failed to operate, Sir William had another ready to stir his readers, namely the love of peace and natural beauty. He tells how in 1623 the *St. Luke* hit upon :—

> "a very pleasant river, and on every side of the same they did see very delicate meadows, having roses white and red growing thereon, with a kind of wild lily with a dainty smell."

Of the second river, which was explored, he wrote :—

> " . . . within this river a very fit place for a plantation, both in regard that it was naturally apt to be fortified, and that all the ground between the two rivers was without wood, and very good fat earth, having several sorts of berries growing thereon, as gooseberries, strawberries, hindberries, raspberries, and a kind of red wineberry, as also some sorts of grain as pease, some ears of wheat, barley and rye. They found likewise in every river abundance of lobsters, cockles and other shell-fishes . . . also several

sorts of wild-fowl, wild goose, black duck, woodcock, crane, heron, pigeon and many other sorts of fowl, which they knew not . . ."

This, it should be noted, was written for a poor country, where dearth, poverty and famine were rampant. It is strange, indeed, that so few Scots rose to such a bait.

And now Alexander rings the change, and appeals to the well-known pride of the Scot :—

"My own countrymen are as fit for such a purpose (of colonising) as any men in the world . . . Scotland, by reason of her populousness being constrained to disburden herself (like the painful bees) did every year send forth swarmes, whereof great numbers did haunt the Pole."

The vision of a glorious Nova Scotia makes the Lieutenant quite rhetorical, as when he asks :—

"Where was ever ambition baited with greater hopes than here, or where ever had virtue so large a field to reap the fruits of glory ? "

But the pious Scot had another card—a trump card—to lay down to win the game. The missionary appeal has always been strong to Scottish hearts, and across the Seven Seas they have roamed to spread the Gospel. Here, pled Alexander, is a great opportunity to convert the heathen and enlarge the Christian Church :—

"Here is a large way of advancing the Gospel of Jesus Christ, to whom churches may be builded in places where his name was never known."

Perhaps the most ambitious feature of the " Encouragement " was its Dedication, which was to no less a person than Charles himself, and he advances even to the king cogent reasons for success :—

" By this means, you that are born to rule nations, enlarging this monarchy without blood, and making a conquest without wronging of others . . . It is a far better course to purchase fame by the plantation of a new world, nor as many princes have done by their desolation of this."

So, altogether, the keen coloniser of the New World made his manifold plea to Scots of all types. But it fell on deaf ears. It was before blind eyes. Even before he had finished his prose pamphlet, it had dawned on him that no private person could be expected to finance a great colonial enterprise, and that public monies of some kind must be forthcoming.

In the midst of this perplexing financial strait, Sir William had to make a diplomatic journey to Rome, and, according to McGrail, the purpose was to secure from the Pope a dispensation to allow the marriage of Charles to Henrietta Maria of France. He was, however, back in Britain by May, 1625, to attend the funeral rites of James. The mission appears to have reached a measure of success, for the wedding by proxy did take place.

In the meanwhile, the famous project of creating Nova Scotia knights was launched. A carefully planned scheme to raise capital for colonising Canada, it was designed also to recoup the impoverished laird of Menstrie. Not for nothing did Alexander remember that Ulster had been planted by James with knights in 1611, and well he knew the royal penchant for creating knights. In 1603 James had made no fewer than 230 knights *en route* for London, and very shortly thereafter he proposed his Order of Golden Knights to subsidise the mining of gold. There was plenty of precedent for the Alexander plan. After consultation with the Privy Council, the complete scheme was proclaimed from the Market Cross of Edinburgh on the 30th November, 1624. Provision was made for 100 knights, who would take precedence of all others— a very touchy point—and whose title would descend by heredity. The wife of the new knight—a sly hook this!— would be styled " Lady," " Madame," " Dame." Later the attraction was increased by the wearing of an orange silk ribbon, carrying a pendant, which flourished the legend :—*Fax mentis honestae gloria.*

But the canny Scots would rise to neither bait nor fly. A few, like Gordon of Lochinvar, and Scot of Scots-tarvet, figured in the order, but the aristocracy and even the pseudo-aristocrats stood aloof. Doubtless, the distance of Nova Scotia was an obstacle. So also was the cool thousand merks, not to mention the six men required to go abroad. But Alexander was willing to meet these difficulties. Another two thousand merks would absolve from finding six men and knights were allowed to take possession of their far-away six thousand acres at Edinburgh Castle by a happy legal fiction! Was ever legal fiction more egregious and bare-faced! At first the titled gentry smiled benignly on the scheme ; then they became jealous and annoyed ; finally, headed by the Earl of Melrose, they angrily protested to the king.

But it was not the wise old fool of Christendom they had to deal with. It was the pertinacious and opinionative Charles. He promptly sacked Melrose and appointed Alexander in his place as Secretary of State. Nor did Charles give the Privy Council peace. In 1627 and 1628 he kept nagging them about securing more knights. Hopes ran high when the 120 ton ship, the *Eagle*, lay in the River Thames, loaded with ordnance for Nova Scotia. Soon it was reported among the knowing ones that Captain Ketch had fallen upon 18 French transports and seized 135 guns—a salutary slap in the face to the encroaching Frenchmen. And then, as if to show his sincere interest in the venture, Alexander sent his own eldest son, his namesake, as Knight Admiral of the whole colony. It was a dear, dear venture, for it cost him the life of his gallant lad. By 1628 four vessels lay off the Scottish coast in a bitter March wind, and embarked seventy tough colonists for Port Royal. True, some recreants took the bounty money and never embarked. But the majority were more honourable. Young Alexander and Lord Ochiltree found, when they arrived in the New World, that the English from New England were sneaking some of the lands of Nova Scotia. It needed all the cunning of the Lieutenant to frustrate their scheme.

It is a measure of the optimism of " the guidman of Menstrie " that in this same year of grace, 1627, he secured from Charles a charter of land in Largs, in order that he might build a large port there for trade with Nova Scotia. He visualised a vast trade opening up with the New World, and, if so, what part of the West coast would be more convenient than Largs ? Sheltered from the south-west gales by the shoulder of the Cumbrae, it was easy of access and convenient for inland traffic. It was a well-conceived adjunct to his colonial scheme. It showed a long term vision. True, this Ayrshire project was given up in 1631, when he sold Largs to John Brisbane for £12,000, but there was good reason for so doing, for Charles had double-crossed his Secretary by bargaining away his valuable colony to the French. In 1627, however, money was urgently needed for the scheme, but all that Alexander got from the Crown were a few pickings from his new post as Keeper of the Signet. This meant that no less than five seals were now in his care, and that no legal document could be authoritative without the Secretary's signature. But every signature involved, naturally, a fee, and every fee was useful to Sir William. It was another little nest-egg for the harassed coloniser!

It is a mystery how the laird of Menstrie survived this severe financial strain. He had no bills of exchange to keep his colonial venture going, and French rivalry was an added strain. Yet on the 30th July, 1628, he could secure the lands and barony of Menstrie, and a year later he added those of Tullibody. Perhaps he expected to retrieve his fortunes by sponsoring a joint-stock company to fish in the West Coast of Scotland, with headquarters on the island of Lewis. If so, he was to learn better very soon. But surer income was to hand than fishing for herring. Already entrusted with the power to appoint Clerks for each shire, Alexander now secured the prerogative of naming the Clerks of the Peace. Here was more power, and sure enough, more pelf! It seemed that every appointment conceivable by royal ingenuity slipped quietly and steadily into Alexander's firm grasp.

Nor was the poet-politician contented with real power without its outward glory. On the 4th of September, 1630, the Privy Council heard that he was now Viscount Stirling and Lord Alexander of Tullibody. So now, as the first Earl of Stirling, he could hold up his head among the highest in the land. But surely the most egregious of all his sinecures was that of the 28th of July, 1631, when Charles made him an Extraordinary Lord of the College of Justice. Though a highly-educated man, "the guidman of Menstrie" was no lawyer and still less a judicial benchman. It was a mere dodge to recoup him for his colonial losses, and as such it was a corrupt practice. Meanwhile, the sedate laird whiled the summer hours away in Menstrie at the expense of the Royal Exchequer, and rather enjoyed playing the local

THE ARGYLE LODGING.

magnate.   Already he had given £50 to the poor of Stirling
to celebrate the return of his son from Nova Scotia.   Now,
to mark his rise to power and fame, the royal burgh of
Stirling conferred on him its freedom.   Archibald
Alexander of Tarbert received the same honour at the
same time.   It was too good a chance to be missed.   Here
was his rival for the chieftainship within a stone's throw of
Menstrie.   He insisted on making his far-away Highland
kinsman his welcome guest, while he played with perfect
aplomb the part of patronising host.   This was the critical
hour when the chieftainship passed into his hands.

It is strange and salutary to note that at this very
moment, when the laird was grasping at such social will-
o'-the-wisps, his son and heir was founding a real empire
beyond the sea.   Fighting bravely against heavy odds,
young Sir William built Fort Granville, whose remains
survive to the present day and are honoured by the sons
of Canada.   By 1632 Charles ordered the Scots to retire
from Port Royal in order to secure from the French the
final instalment of the marriage dowry for Henrietta Maria,
but the claim to Nova Scotia was never revoked or resigned
by Scotland, so that in the end the son did better work than
his father.   The fact is that the perplexed Secretary of
State was getting somewhat tired of his vast empire, and
by 1632 he was glad to get out of it with an " I.O.U."
from Charles for £10,000.   He should have known better
than trust a paper promise from Charles.   The grant was
never paid to him by the king, and McGrail informs us
that the Alexanders tried unsuccessfully to get it right up
to 1832.

Did this colonial failure discourage Sir William?
Not a bit!   His many appointments produced a steady
income, and his running expenses were met by the
Exchequer.   He devised his coat-of-arms in 1632 and

c

commissioned Marshall to paint his portrait. Posterity should know what like he looked. He rebuilt and enlarged Menstrie Castle, and soon set his jealous eye on Tillicoultry, which he acquired on the 12th of July, 1634. But before this he figured in the brilliant coronation of Charles at Holyrood in 1633, and this might be termed the pinnacle and peak of his strange, meteoric career. The king showed the fullness of his royal favour by investing him as the Earl of Stirling and Viscount of Canada although the patent had been granted three years previously. He had reached his highest ambition. Life could scarcely give him more. Certain it is that from this point onwards he met little but discouragements, difficulties and disasters.

All he needed now to complete his social prestige was a town house in Stirling. His son Anthony was a skilled architect. He would design a house worthy of the Alexanders. And he did. Sure enough a noble mansion arose close to the Castle entrance and well above the tall, thin tenements of the Scots nobility. Its mullionedwindows and balanced proportions, its crows-steps without and its panelled walls within, were calculated to delight the most critical eye. And well set above the doorway, the coat of arms added the aristocratic touch. The legend was well chosen, *Per Mare, Per Terras*. Even in this triumphant hour his evil fate pursued him, and dashed the bitter aloes in his cup, for some merry fellow placed a piece of calico over the legend with the facetious alteration, *Per Metre Per Turners*. Nor was there any lack of shrewdness in the jest. It was poetry that brought the quiet scholar of Menstrie into royal favour. But what bodes the Turners?

This was the colloquial name for the copper coin circulating in Scotland in 1631. Some think it derives from *Turnois*, the French term for a coin minted in Tours.

It became, however, as inflammatory as a red rag to a bull
on a Scots lip, for it signified chicanery and deception
practised on the poor. But let's be fair. Scotland had
need of a small coin for household purchases. Charles
realised the need, so he authorised 1500 stone-weight of
copper to be made into coins. The trouble started when
the king saw in this a chance to repay Alexander some of
the £16,000 he owed him. So he gave to his Secretary
for nine years the monopoly of minting the copper.
Menstrie rubbed his hands in happy expectation. He
issued a hundred thousand farthings—according to John
Gordon of Rothiemay—and gave them the value of two-
pence. The result was inflation and privation for the poor.
Soon the mention of " Turners " brought curses from a
dozen lips, and Alexander was execrated, justly or unjustly.
And so the calico legend at the Castle entrance raised
many a raucous guffaw from the crowd. The calico was
soon ripped off and the joke passed away, but not the grace-
ful mansion that tops the long ascent to the Castle. Still
it stands, a beautiful monument to the Alexanders, whose
genius and over-reaching vanity brought it into being,
even though to-day, by a strange irony, Argyle has dis-
placed the very name of Alexander.

The Earl of Stirling settled in his new abode, where
the poetic muse returned to visit him for a short season.
He re-issued his " Recreations with the Muses," but with
a furtive look at some Biblical passages the muse deserted
him. The poetic fire was dying. The urge was gone.

Not indeed that interest and passion had deserted
the political field. On the contrary, Stirling was now
dealing with explosive material, the dearly bought religion
of the common people. It is well known that James
tried to provide his subjects with a better metrical version
of the Psalms for public worship. Even from this,

Alexander planned to draw some financial benefit. Charles gave him the monopoly of publishing these Psalms for twenty-one years and make what profit he could on the venture. And why not? For Alexander himself had translated most of these for James. But the General Assembly would have none of Menstrie's florid renderings of the staid and solemn Hebrew. It scoffed for instance at :—

> " Yon flaming Lord of Light
> And with the stars in state
> Pale Lady of the Night."

This was more than the grim Scot, face to face with his God, could stomach. The bishops were powerless.

But the situation became really serious when Laud's Liturgy was foisted on the people, and by a second blunder Alexander's Psalms were bound in the same volume, so that when Jenny Geddes rejected the Liturgy she meant to reject also the Psalms of Menstrie.

And with the Psalms went the author. For he was not only the instrument of Charles but himself also a stout Episcopalian, an out-and-out king's man, a suspect in the eyes of Presbytery. He had tried to placate the Church by giving it land in Menstrie and Gogar in 1634, but churchmen were not so easily bribed. The wonder is that a shrewd mind like that of Alexander did not gauge better the temper of the Scot. He could hardly have been ignorant, had he walked along a Stirling street, of the smouldering resentment that was to break in fury at the Assembly of 1638 and to bid defiance to the king himself. He knew—and knew only too well— on what side his bread was buttered, and the royal hand that larded it so thickly. It is baffling to think that with all his political shrewdness he had part and lot in the gravest political blunder in all British history.

It was now that blow followed blow. He dared not show himself in Scotland for fear of the infuriated mob, and he was obliged to appoint his eldest surviving son to assist him in his duties. But in September, 1637, Sir Anthony, his second son, suddenly died, while in May of the next year Sir William, the apple of his eye, the real and gallant planter of Nova Scotia, died in London of a fever which was alleged to be the result of his colonising activities. The acerbity of his grief was assuaged somewhat by a brave and manly letter from Drummond of Hawthornden. And worse disasters were round the corner. The Bishop's War now put upon Alexander the colour not only of suspicion but even treason. The General Assembly seriously considered preferring no less than forty charges against the king's courtier.

These and other factors sounded like the tolling of the bell for " the guidman of Menstrie," and he strove to set his house in order. Already Charles had made him Earl of Doven (Devon), in order that all his possessions at death would go with his title, and now in 1639 all his American properties were included in a fresh charter. He was indeed deeply concerned that neither his title nor his family should die out. His fond ambition was to found a Scottish house, and like Scott he sacrificed solvency itself to attempt it. He little knew that posterity would belie his burning hope, for both titles and property are no more and his family faded from the public ken.

Such meticulous care against the ravages of time were but premonitions of the end. The man was sick unto death. By January, 1640, Traquar reported that he was not expected to live and by the 12th of February on his bed at Covent Garden he was a dead man. The *Dictionary of National Biography* and the *Scottish Nation* give the date of death as 12th September, 1640, but Paul's

Scots Peerage, Vol. viii, p. 175, Sir James Balfour, *Annales of Scotland*, Vol. ii, p. 427, and T. H. McGrail, p. 185, give February. But not before his agitated creditors crowded round his bed and demanded his signature to the assignment of his emoluments. They might have saved their breath, their paper and their quills. When the account was closed, it was found that he owed the world no less than two hundred thousand merks Scots, while the world owed him a bare ten thousand pounds. He died a hopeless bankrupt.

This, of course, did not prevent a worthy funeral. His body was embalmed before leaving London and carried by ship up the east coast to the Forth. The earl came home to the royal burgh from which he took his title, and he who feared to tread it alive came to it at last in the panoply of death. They planned to bury his leaden coffin under cover of darkness in Bowie's Aisle of the High Kirk of Stirling on the 12th of April. This had been carefully designed by the astute earl some twenty-two years before, when he had bought the space and Sir Anthony had planned a vault below and a family pew above. But it was all to no purpose. Creditors faced the coffin at the very door of the church and denied it burial. For a hundred years it lay outside the Church, and the lead of the unburied coffin was a quarry for schoolboys' pencils. In 1812, the Aisle was finally demolished and the dust of the mighty earl was scattered to the four winds of heaven.

His was a strange and chequered career. That he had surpassing gifts cannot be questioned. His vast learning, his great and sustained literary powers, his courteous manner, his diplomatic skill and his personal drive and determination, all fitted him excellently for a high and noble part in public affairs. These gifts he developed to their utmost and these he used most skilfully, but only for the glory of himself and his house. His weakness was complete and unbridled selfishness, and to this he consecrated every thought and action. He bowed the knee to an earthly god and found, all too late, that it betrayed him. Better for him far to have lived quietly in his modest mansion at Menstrie among his books and his kindly country neighbours. There he could drink each day of the pure waters of the glen, and there, too, he could drink of the deep fount of poesy. As the wise " guidman " of the village, he would have lived in peace and died in honour. But it was not to be. He chose a different ideal and bitterly he reached it.

Two claims he has upon the modern age ; a handful of chaste and memory-haunting sonnets and the vision of a great dominion across the Atlantic.

BIBLIOGRAPHY

Sir WILLIAM ALEXANDER—
An encouragement to colonies. 1624. Ed. David Laing. 1867.
The poetical works of Sir William Alexander. Ed. L. E. Kastner and H. B. Charlton. 2 vols. 1921-9.
The Earl of Stirling's register of royal letters relative to the affairs of Scotland and Nova Scotia, 1615-1635. Ed. Charles Rogers. 2 vols. 1884-5.

E. F. SLAFTER—
Sir William Alexander and American colonization. 1865.
The copper coinage of the Earl of Stirling, 1632. 1874.

CHARLES ROGERS—
Memorials of the Earl of Stirling and of the House of Alexander. 2 vols. 1877.

T. H. McGRAIL—
Sir William Alexander, the first Earl of Stirling. 1940.

GEORGE PRATT INSH—
Scottish colonial schemes, 1620-1686. 1922.

CHAPTER II

BOBBING JOHN OF THE 'FIFTEEN

IT will always be known as Mar's Rising, despite the detractors. Never by any chance could it be named the Pretender's Invasion, for he arrived after it was launched and fled before it was over. John, the sixth Earl of Mar, was its soul and inspiration. While others grumbled and talked loudly of rebellion, he it was who raised the standard and summoned the clansmen to rally round it. He had more to lose than any other of the Jacobite nobility, and while Seafield, Huntly and Cromarty quibbled and criticised, he took decisive action and gambled everything on the venture. And in this dramatic *volte face* he had to eat more of his own words and contradict more of his own career than any other public man in the whole land. Some may deride his generalship at Sheriffmuir ; others may doubt his political sincerity, but the whole of the 'Fifteen was Mar's affair both in its fame and its failure.

He was nicknamed Bobbing John. A certain nervous twitching of the head suggested the term. The fact that he was slightly deformed, though not apparent in portraits of him, is beyond doubt, and this gains colour from the deformity of his sister Jean, the wife of Sir Hugh Paterson of Bannockburn, for she was a hunch-back. The soubriquet came from the bobbing motion of John's body and not from his behaviour in politics, for after all, he made only one change in his political front. He suffered obloquy and even blows for his policy of Union, and in his last days he refused a pension from Stair, all because he would not change his politics.

This was the Erskine who was born at Alloa House in 1675. The family fortunes were low, but not so low as to deny John a good education in Edinburgh, a further course at the University of Leyden in Holland, and all the thrills of the Grand Tour. His political line had in a sense been defined for him by his father, who in 1688 had sided with William, and it was a matter of course that John should acknowledge him as the rightful monarch. Endowed with more ambition and ability than his father, John took his seat in the Scottish Parliament in 1696 and the very next year was appointed to the Privy Council. In 1699 he was appointed, like all the Earls of Mar, as governor of Stirling Castle. He was created a Knight of the Thistle in 1706.

The highest office of all he attained was Secretary, and no man rises to be Secretary of State for Scotland without manifest gifts. Mar was a man of affairs. Macky in his Secret Memoirs was right in stating, " He is a very good manager of his private affairs, which were in disorder when his father died, and is a staunch country-man, fair complexioned, low stature and thirty years old." With the foundation of a good academic training the sixth earl was able to enter the field of politics and gain from the Duke of Queensberry an excellent apprentice-ship in the craftsmanship of state. Indeed, one of the most beautiful things in his life was the tender and un-clouded friendship that grew between these two public personalities. Mar's letter to his brother Grange des-cribing Queensberry's death is inimitable. " . . . he died sn handsomely, both like a gentleman and a Christian, that 'twere pity you did not know it . . . he desired the sacrament might be prepared for him, and in the time they were adoing that, he took leave of all his friends present . . . and then died without any pain or concern, but like one going a journey." When the powerful duke fell out of the race with ill-health, Mar was the obvious leader of the party, and he drove straight ahead with the policy of welding England and Scotland together. It seemed the only line to take in days when the political fabric was shaking. The swift successions of William, of Mary and of Anne left men wondering who would follow next and Mar knew only too intimately the plots beneath the surface to restore the direct line of the Stuarts. And this brought out the ruling trait in the man.

Mar had the flair of the architect. This emerged early when he set about to re-build the fortunes of his house. He called in a very celebrated architect, named James Gibb, to enlarge his house at Alloa, and so generously did he recognise his gifts and so helpful was he with introductions, that James Gibb bequeathed all his wealth to the Erskine children as a mark of his gratitude. The Earl had a great love for his place. While he enhanced the building, he did not forget the gardens, for he engaged the famous gardener of Louis XIV, Le Notre, to come over and plan his grounds. How he loved those gardens ! In the leafy month of June, 1708, he was recalled to London, and only a sense of duty tore him unwillingly from Alloa. When an invasion had threatened from France in March, 1708, Mar, trembling in Whitehall, thought first of his garden, " I hope neither friends nor enemies will be so barbarous as to spoil my gardens." The family fortunes, too, benefited from Mar's architectural urge. He lost no chance of increasing the income of the family, for he kept claiming for the expenses of even his office, as Secretary of State, and when Queen Anne died in 1714 he claimed no less than £7,000 as owing to him by the State. Anne, herself, had settled a pension on him of £3,000 during her lifetime. In those days, this was big money and John could not but feel he was a builder.

But Mar was supremely the architect of the Union. To him more than to any other is due the accomplishment of this difficult task. Rait, the Scottish historian, attributes most of Scotland's prosperity and progress to that Union, but in 1706 it was anything but apparent. Mar was the pilot of the measure through the Scottish Parliament, and if he soon rued his pro-Union enthusiasm, his sublime faith has in the end been justified. It was he who placed the draft before his compatriots and fought for it clause by clause. His correspondence proves how unweariedly he carried on the campaign day after day. This dogged persistence showed him at his finest. How tactfully and shrewdly he handled the difficult Scots members of the House! His prestige was at its highest. Negotiating for union in London in 1703 he wrote to his brother James, the imperturbable Lord Grange, " For my own share, I'm very well just now at court, but you know that's a slippery place. The Union succeeds pretty well, but slowly. I believe they will conclude most of the articles, and really the English are fair enough hitherto . . . I'm afraid we spoil it ourselves ; but by what I can learn the generality of the English nation are for it, and some time or other we'll have it." The next year, feeling himself no doubt in the swim of affairs, he told his wife, " People pays (sic) court to me . . . I wish they may not find themselves mistaken." As Secretary of State, too, Mar was well aware of the impending Jacobite invasions. Argyll warned him in 1705 of the ship St. Paul's leaving Dunkirk with five or six men of war and making for Scotland with arms, ammunition and money.

Bobbing John had, as a matter of fact, a stiff battle against many enemies. A crumb of comfort came his way occasionally, as when the Earl of Marchmont told him in 1705, " I have known and esteemed you very long for the probity, worth and ingenuity I have ever discerned in you," but there was opposition to the measure both open and secret. The underground activities of the Catholics and many Episcopalians, the deep emotional sympathies of the Stuart connections, the little Scotland-ism of the rabble of Edinburgh, all combined to undo his efforts. Only a master in the handling of men could have driven so controversial a measure through Parliament. Nor were all the opponents of union dishonest men. Some were honest-to-goodness fellows, who just did not like and did not trust the English. Outspoken characters like Saltoun cursed it to Mar as "a damned villainous Union," although once it was passed Cromarty expressed a furtive hope ; " Unless we be part of each other, the union will be as a blood pudding to bind the cat, and till one or the other be hungry, and then the pudding flies. God give all of you prudence, wisdom and honesty and British minds. May we be Britons, and down go the old ignominious name of Scotland or England." Dupplin, Stair and Leven all gave him their moral support and he needed it. The first stage of the battle was reached when he reported to his wife in September, 1705, " The Act I presented was passed not having almost a word altered." The stability of the whole country depended on Mar, and he shook at the thought that no cannon powder could be found in Edinburgh Castle and only 2,000 old firelocks, while in Stirling Castle there were no beds for the soldiers to lie on. He knew that the Presby-terians were joining the Jacobites against the Union, that the Articles of Union had been burned at the Cross of Stirling on 4th December, 1706, by the mob, and with his own eyes he saw the Edinburgh toughs drinking the

health of the Pretender. Indeed, he had told Whitehall on
19th November, 1706, " I'm not very timorous and
yet I tell you that every day here we are in hazard of
our lives. We cannot go on the streets, but we are in-
sulted, as I and some others just now . . ." Bobbing
John had, clearly, just escaped the mob and wanted to tell
London about it, while it was fresh in his mind ! Wild
rumours, too, were spreading that James was on the
point of landing in the Highlands with a cadre of 200
officers and, to persuade the wavering, that he had turned
Protestant. Only a man of stern courage and indomitable
purpose could have held to his unpopular course, in the
face of these daunting difficulties, and the sixth Earl of
Mar deserves, for this alone, to be classed as a statesman
of the first rank. The Queen had very good reason to
thank him in 1707, after both Parliaments had passed
the Union, in such cordial words : " The pains you have
taken in bringing this great affair about deserves more
thanks than I am able to express." Anne was shrewd
enough and Scot enough to see in union the only hope
for her throne. With the pride of the architect in his
completed structure Mar dashed off to London on the
20th of March, 1707, his proudest sentence : " God be
thankt this great and good work is now so happily concluded."

This was his happiest and most successful hour.
He could look back upon a supremely difficult task
triumphantly carried through. Well he knew that underground contacts were being maintained with the Pretender
at St. Germains, that the crafty old Louis XIV was
planning a swoop on Britain, that men like Kinnoull, his
own father-in-law, were at heart Jacobites. Queensberry
told him of the movements of Colonel Nathaniel Hooke,
who passed to and fro between France and the Highlands.

It was all this knowledge that made Mar mighty glad to have the Union realised as an accomplished fact. He had good reason to be happy.

And yet almost from the very month of Union the star of John Erskine seemed to decline. On that very day, the 20th of March, he told the Queen that he had been " in the country seeing my poor wife, who I fear is adying," and sure enough, while he was attending to matters of state at Whitehall on 2nd May, 1707, the heavy news reached him that she was dead. This change in his private life was matched by equally drastic changes in the political set-up. The Duke of Ormonde represented the interests of James at Court, but he was dismissed from the important post of Lord Lieutenant of Ireland. True, John himself was later appointed Secretary of State for Scotland in Whitehall, and this caused him no little satisfaction. But who else was in the running? His claims for the post were unrivalled. If he thought his troubles were over, he was much mistaken. Harry Maule and his brother, Lord Grange, kept him well informed of the pulse of the country, and it soon became apparent that if feeling was bitter before the passing of the Act of Union, it was more bitter afterward. Maule told him in June, 1707, " The people in the west are so obstinate still in their inveterate temper against the Union that rather than submit to it they'll assist King James." So united were the Presbyterians and Episcopalians in their opposition to union with England that Grange told his brother at this time, " Church and Kirk are at bottom much of the same kidney." When the Darien Company shares fell some 12 to 15 per cent. in a few weeks' time, Colonel Stewart told Mar that this was a clear reflection of how the Scots doubted the loathsome alliance. Three months later Grange added to his worries by repeating the Edinburgh rumour that Athole, Breadalbane and Drummond were plotting an insurrection in the Highlands. And it was more than a rumour, shortly afterwards, that twenty-two battalions of troops were marshalled at Dunkirk, ready to swoop down on Scotland. He posted north to the capital, and was soon at pains to inform the Queen that the people of Scotland were against the Union. With his own eyes he saw the infuriated crowds of the capital unafraid and in public drinking treasonably to the Pretender's health! Here indeed was a strange world for the pillar of society! He could be forgiven for comforting himself with a snatch of poetry, as he did a little later :—

"Gramashes above and galashes below,
    It's a wonder to see how this world does go."

But these overt moves against both him and his Union did not affect him so deeply as the cunning political intrigue that now shewed its hand. Elections were going ahead in Scotland in 1708, not without malice and even corruption. The enemies of Mar were securing the ear of the Queen and whispering there the worst they could, so the Secretary wrote boldly to her majesty, "I must say that the endeavours used by some people to discourage and bear down those who made the Union here, and joining with the opposers against them, give people here strange notion of it." The iron is beginning to enter into the soul of Mar. It was a disadvantage to him to be obliged to live at Privy Garden in London at such a time, but his devoted brother was a splendid listening-post for him, and kept him accurately informed of the swing of feeling in Scotland. He could hardly be blamed for squaring off his debt by making him on 27th July, 1710, the Lord Justice Clerk. It was unfortunate for John that he had to fight both a vanguard and a rearguard action, and little did he reckon at this time that it was

JOHN, SIXTH EARL OF MAR, K.T.
(By kind permission of the Rt. Hon. The Earl of Mar and Kellie).

the rearguard action of political spite and blackmail that was to overthrow him.

After the Union a great game of negotiation began. The first disappointment was the affront to the Scots peerage. The English lords refused them seats in the Upper House. How it cut Mar to the quick! It made the Scotsmen to a man bitter and resentful and made all Mar's former pleadings appear as so much base treachery. The wrangling of the peers wearied even the English, and John, almost half-hopefully comments, " The English, as most of the Scots, seem to be wearie of the Union, but when they first come to think of it seriously, I doubt of their quitting with it." We know now that the humiliating compromise was reached, whereby Scotland elected only sixteen peers to sit in London, but neither at that time nor to-day has this been acceptable to Scots sentiment. It was this cavalier treatment that swayed the sympathies of the disappointed Scots statesman. We can put our finger on the very day when he changed. It was January 17th, 1711/12, when he wrote to his brother, " What we can do God knows, and I wish He may direct us. To go peaceably home and rebel, as the Irishman said, is but a bad remedy, and yet it is impossible for us to lay under this hardship. If we saw a possibility of getting free of the Union without a civil war we would have some comfort, but that I'm afraid is impossible." Here is the seed-thought that English truculence, political intrigue and German boorishness were to nurture into a bitter herb. In the same letter he confessed that he had been grievously disappointed in the results of the Union, but he scouts the idea, then prevalent in the north, that the Union could be easily dissolved in a constitutional fashion. In the thick of the machinery of State he just could not conceive such an expedient. In other words, only civil war could

D

undo the deed.   On the one side, the English refused power
to the Scots, lest the Queen become too strong; on the
other, the Scots were straining at the leash of civil war;
and Mar was caught in a cleft stick.

Before charges of disloyalty are hurled against men
of the calibre of the Earl of Mar, it is well to realise that
many people in Scotland felt free to call the Pretender to
the Scottish throne in perfect good faith.   The Act of
Settlement of 1701 was passed only by the English, and
this tied the hands of the southern kingdom to the house
of Hanover.   Mary had died and Anne had now no heir
surviving, so that there was no hope of issue in that quarter,
and the Act explicitly provided that Hanover would
succeed.   But the Scots did not so tie their hands.   Even
the Act of Security of 1704 made large qualifications to
accepting the House of Hanover.   They felt themselves
free to revert to the original Stuart line, and many, quite
wrongly, in good faith felt free to choose whichever option
they deemed best.   None knew this more clearly than Mar,
and it is little wonder that his bitter experiences in Whitehall
turned his mind to the other option of recalling the Pretender.   Looking back, after the Rising was over and
done with, he told his son: " When I found that we
continued to be ill-treated under the Union, I became
as much for having it broke as ever I had been for having
it made . . .   I found the breaking of it impossible
without an entire revolution by restoring our Natural
King, to whose family I had always had a heart's liking.
This made me enter into a correspondence with the king
about the time of the change of ministry the last years of
Queen Anne."

Thus we have the strange spectacle of a trusted pillar
of the State, no less than a Secretary of State, playing the
double role.   If this appears to us to be highly reprehensible

it should be noted that Ormonde, Oxford, Bolingbroke and others were playing the same game, and it is curious to note that modern historians like the Taylers villify Mar, not for invidiously serving two masters, but for serving James so tardily. The fact is that public men in that changing age of Anne were caught on the horns of a fearful dilemma, and counsels of moral perfection failed to deliver them. As it was, Bobbing John was in a good position to study the key agents who passed between the Pretender at St. Germains and his sympathisers and to gauge the support that Louis would throw into the field at the critical moment. The movements of Jacobite spies were constantly reported to him, and well he knew that Union was raising the tempo and swelling the flood of Jacobite sentiment. When the Chevalier de St. George made his unlucky descent on the east coast in 1708, the names of the principal insurgents were known at once to Mar, who, not yet disillusioned by the English, lent his knowledge to the government.

This double loyalty, each in its own way sincere enough, made Mar and more than Mar anticipate the *dénouement*, when Anne should die. Then would strike the hour for deciding whether a Stuart or a Hanoverian would mount the throne. And the more the loyal Scots knew the English the less they liked George. To them it was an open question, and each was ready to spring either way. And die Anne did. In a matter of days she sickened and died and events got out of hand. Things moved too speedily for the slow and cautious Erskine. Overnight the whole political scene changed. Only the Duke of Buckingham had the quick wit to see the fleeting chance of the Jacobites, for he warned Ormonde that there were only twenty-four hours in which to effect the turnover. It is clear from Mar's long letter to his brother of August

7th, 1714, that he was too undecided to strike the blow for James. " Though I say it who should not, I can make as good terms with the other side as any of them, and I will not be made the fool of the play; though they shall not have me to complain of first." And what perplexed John still more was the hard, financial fact that the State owed him a cool seven thousand pounds. This would make any man think twice. He bluntly asserts that what concerns him most is to have his arrears paid. And he has some reason to tremble even for his arrears. " I know very well," he writes to his brother, " people have been at pains to represent me very unfavourably to the King for some years past, but as that was all calumny and out of party designs, he will find in time that there was nothing in it; and one prince seldom likes a man the worse for serving his predecessor faithfully and with zeal." But this was nothing more than bolstering up his courage. The fateful twenty-four hours had fled and James had missed his chance. Within a week Mar knew the die was cast. " Jacobitism," he wrote, " is now, I presume, out of doors."

But worse was to come. For some time he had noticed that the Hanoverian ministers, while paying their courtesies to all the other government heads, had studiously avoided the Secretary for Scotland. It stung his noble Scottish pride. He dared even to tell the Queen about it. She advised restraint and patience and counselled him to avoid them. How he longed for the firm grasp of German that his clever brother James possessed, and he would tell these Hanoverians the truth! He would even explain to the King himself. But if speech were denied, there was pen and paper to hand. He sat down on August 30th and drew up an address to the new king, still in Hanover. This adduced proof to George of his good

faith. Had he not more than other men, guided the
Act of Union to success, had the Erskines for centuries
not been loyal to their acknowledged monarchs, did he
not promise devotion to George with his hand on his
heart? But the only reaction from Hanover was to
demand his Seals of Office. So the poison had worked!
The new king hated him. His days of power were num-
bered. His enemies had got in first. Poor Mar could
hardly believe it. For a whole year he hoped against
hope that George would give him a fair trial and let him
prove his worth and fidelity. And then the crushing blow
fell. True, the proclamation of George as monarch of
Britain was challenged by a broadside from James, but
it was from no nearer than Plombieres, and the Whigs
replied with an offer of £100,000 for the arrest of the
Pretender. The Hanoverian landed on the 18th of
September, and but for the faint echo from Devon of
James III's proclamation, all was quiet in his new kingdom.
John Erskine saw he had to watch his step, for he still
hoped to win the good graces of the German Elector.
A levee was to be held on the first of August, 1715. Sus-
picions had been falling upon him for some time. He
felt eyes watching him. He had a sense of being
" covered." But he would make one last throw. He
would present himself at the levee. And so he went.
George snubbed him in public! He could hardly believe
it. The affront cut him to the core. It was the rudest
of insults to a great public servant, and neither his inno-
cence of English nor his ignorance of British ways can
excuse the king. In the event, it was not only a breach
of etiquette but a political blunder of the first magnitude,
for out of it came in the end not only the 'Fifteen but also
the 'Forty-Five Risings.

The rest can be logically deduced. In a single

day, the able and adroit Mar swung right across the political
front and aligned himself and his fortunes with the old
Scottish House of Stuart. And had he, now, any real
alternative? When he had reached the safe fastnesses
of Braemar, and not till then, he explained to his brother
James, in writing why he disappeared from London: " I
found that I could continue no longer at London with
my liberty, for I had certain information that I was one of
those to be very quickly taken up, and though I knew
of no crime I was guilty of, I thought it high time to see
to my own liberty now when it is in their power to imprison
for what time they think fit anybody they are pleased to
suspect; and in those times dislike is commonly thought
ground enough for suspicion." In other words, he would
have been jailed and hung had he stayed another day in
London. Had not Bolingbroke and Ormonde fled just
in time to France, the latter with hardly a shirt to his
back? In less than twenty-four hours Bobbing John
was aboard a little collier at Gravesend, dressed as a
deck-hand and accompanied by Major-General Hamilton,
and bound for St. Andrews in Fife. It belonged, in fact,
to John Spence of Leith and boasted of but two seamen.
Their " get-away " was well planned and escaped suspicion. It was when they landed at Elie—for St. Andrews
was not feasible—that they were tracked. So high was
the sea that Mar's chief servant fell off the plank into the
sea and so was drowned. On they sped across Fife to
spend the night with Kinnoull, John's new father-in-law, at
Perth. Little did they reckon that a spy was covering
them as they pressed on to Rattray of Blairgowrie, and
even in Strathardle the informer stopped to count the
cavalcade of eighteen horsemen as they clattered by. The
very words he used to persuade Ashentullie to throw
in his lot with the Jacobites were soon heard in Whitehall,

and George must have smirked with satisfaction to know that Farquharson of Invercauld had bluntly denied Mar's right to be commander. Undaunted by this, John roused the country by telling the wives that the wicked Hanoverians were set on taxing even the very cocks and hens, and, much more successfully, he organised a Hunting Party at Braemar for August 27th. It was merely a euphemism. The Jacobite chieftains rolled up for the Party and were shewn Mar's Commission from James III and VIII. Sinclair, " The Devil in the Camp," roundly declared it a fake. The Taylers may be right in suggesting that it was a draft drawn up by Mar until the original arrived from James, but the Commission published in the Mar and Kellie Papers, dated at Bar-le-Duc the 7th of September, 1715, does not designate Mar as the Commander-in-Chief; it merely designates him a " councillor " and the space for the commander is left blank !

The fact is that Mar faced the surprised James with a *fait accompli*. He cut right across whatever plans Berwick, Ormonde and the St. Germains group were making, and this he knew quite well. It was, in fact, far more than his " heart's liking ; " it was his only hope of a whole skin. Indeed, tendentious writers like the Taylers may be forgiven for their systematic discrediting of Mar, who in their eyes only ruined an excellent opportunity of re-instating the Stuarts on the throne. But the position was better known to Mar than to the French Jacobites, or, for that matter, to the Taylers of to-day. Mar knew that Stirling Castle did not possess five barrels of gunpowder and Edinburgh had barely 2,000 flintlocks. He knew that the French king would not give a penny to help the Jacobites. He knew that Berwick was doing nothing and could do nothing. Already a year had been lost since Anne died and the longer the delay the cooler would be the Highland enthusiasm. Such a situation coincided with his own desperate political dilemma, and although he had no authority whatever from James himself, he crossed his Rubicon and gambled on the throw.

And so on the 6th of September, 1715, before a company of six hundred supporters, he unfurled the banner of the Pretender. And a beautiful banner it was. The new Lady Mar, still in the enthusiasm of her first year of married life, had wrought it on blue silk. On one side the Scottish arms sparkled in gold, and on the other the patriotic Thistle, the inseparable legend *Nemo Me Impune Lacessit*, and with truculent brevity No Union. Attached to the standard were two pennants of white ribbon, displaying For Our Wronged King and Oppressed Country and For Ourselves and Liberties. The letters " JR " accompanied by several figures appear also to have been inscribed. It was a brave display, and would have thrilled the beholders, if the gilt ball had not, most inauspiciously, fallen from the top of the standard. To some it was an ill omen. But Mar rose above such trifling incidents and facing the eager Jacobites he spoke at great length on the aims of the rising, and proved himself " a wonderfully persuasive speaker." This is true. John Erskine was brilliantly persuasive, for did he not win over such powerful chiefs as Huntly, Tullibardine, Mareschal, Southesk, Glengarry, Glendaruel, Linlithgow, Drummond, Panmure, Kinnoull and many others ? His letter to Black Jock Forbes of Kildrummie is an excellent sample of his technique. He shames the wavering tenants with, " And now when the . . . country's cause is at stake, will they for ever sit still and see all perish ? ", but he goes on to apply stronger pressure, " I will send a party immediately to burn . . ."

And so the clansmen came in. From Braemar

he moved his forces down to the Spittal of Glenshee, and up Strathardle to Kirkmichael, where eight hundred more Highlanders joined him. This induced him to unfurl the glorious banner again and issue a rousing Proclamation. Over the hill to the Vale of Athole and down by the hospitable inn at Moulin he led his gathering forces, and cheered them with the news that Perth had already been taken by Colonel John Hay, and that soon they would be masters in Edinburgh and so on to England, where the rightful king would be before them. Once at Perth John ordered the cannon to be sent on from Dunnottar and Dundee and all the bullets and gunpowder from Montrose. He made Perth his headquarters, and by the end of September some four to five thousand insurgents occupied the town.

This was the critical hour. If he had rushed his eager forces south to Stirling, before Argyll with a mere 1200 soldiers reached it, Scotland would have been lying at his feet. Doubtless he had to placate the various chieftains' interests, and some leaders were slow to come in. " The great Montrose," say the Taylers, " given Mar's forces and opportunities, would have won Scotland for his master in three weeks." It is at any rate significant that the attempts at Edinburgh Castle, Burntisland, Dunfermline and Northumberland all petered out, and as these were nominally under the command of Mar, he has been obliged to bear the blame. Even so, he was now strongly placed in Perth with at least 16,000 men, while Argyll, gathering troops as he went, was pressing forward to Stirling with barely 4,000. It was clear that if the standard of the Pretender was ever to wave in English air, Argyll must be cleared out of the way. So southward the insurgents pressed. The plan of Mar was to attack Stirling at three points, so splitting the meagre forces of

Argyll, but he found that Argyll had pushed rapidly forward from Stirling and captured Dunblane, and camped his forces on the hill above the town in the direction of Sheriffmuir. Mar, on hearing this news from a lame boy sent by Mrs. Stirling of Kippendavie, pushed forward to Kinbuck, and waited for the dawn. It was a Sunday morning—the 13th of November, doubly unlucky perhaps, when Bobbing John saw Argyll's forces drawn up in their selected positions. Although the left wing, after an impetuous assault, was driven down to the river Allan, with sore loss of wounded, the right centre, under John himself, was triumphantly successful and chased the enemy to Causewayhead. The right wing of the Jacobites remained intact, waiting for orders that never came, and the end of the day saw two forces facing each other on the moor, each afraid to commit itself to final victory or defeat.

Although Mar had been the Commanding Officer of a regiment under Queen Anne, it is undoubted that he lacked the dash and spirit of a soldier, and he is seen probably at his worst in the Battle of Sheriffmuir. But let it not be forgotten that Argyll was little better. The contour of the ground, too, must be reckoned on, for the hills, glens and rivers turned it almost into a blind battle. The fact remains, however, that Argyll returned to the battlefield unchallenged and gathered such trophies as remained, while Mar pressed north to Ardoch and Perth. If the battle did not crush the Rising it certainly changed the tactics, and compelled the commander to fall back on the prestige of James's presence to rally the dispirited Jacobites for another march south. Once back in his snug room at Perth, he penned an epistle to his king—he was much better with the pen than with the sword—and assured his majesty that his presence in Scotland would give new life to the cause. He covered up cleverly his handling of the battle, but the letter frankly warned James of a deteriorating situation before he landed on the coast. Nevertheless, land on the coast the king did. He came ashore at Peterhead, and two days later, at the door of Fetteresso Castle, on 24th December, he was proclaimed the true king. Now he knew the melancholy truth, nor did it dispel his temperamental morbidity.

His state entry into Perth on 9th January, 1716, added a much-needed glamour to the whole adventure, and the attempt to conduct a royal court at Scone served to lend a spurious kind of authority to the Rising, but it clearly could not survive long in this artificial atmosphere. A handful of episcopal clergy might swear devotion to him, but the clansmen were steadily disappearing back to their Highland fastnesses. A month of the stage-play was enough. Argyll was advancing, and by the end of the month James and Mar and the insurgents were heading for Montrose. There they abandoned the ragged remnants of the Jacobites, who, while a little ship carried their king and commander to France, hurried on to Aberdeen and Ruthven in Badenoch, whence they dispersed to their chosen hiding-places. By the 15th of February the tragic episode was closed and the ten remaining leaders were asking Argyll for honourable terms. The 'Fifteen was over.

Not so the resourceful Bobbing John. There is a sense, indeed, in which he now revealed his greatest and most fascinating qualities. The old flair of the architect, which had displayed itself in his making of the Union, was inoperative in the destructive activities of war. He, who could be so persuasive with tongue and pen, was unfitted for the more brutal exercise of the sword. He could not build kingdoms, even in the air, on the bloody field of battle. Now that the battles were over, the architect in him set to work again. Even the biographer of Argyll, writing later, was compelled to admit of Mar, "He was an able statesman and wanted not personal courage." Even James credited him with probity and experience and because of this took Earl John with him on the *Marie Therese* to Waldam, near Gravelines in France. Already he had created him a Duke, and now made him succeed Bolingbroke as his Secretary of State and First Gentleman of the Bed-Chamber. He thus became the very centre of the whole Stuart intrigue and carried on an immense correspondence. Denied hospitality at St. Germains, James moved his court to Avignon, but after ten months he was forced to move to Rome, where under the protection and patronage of the Pope he tried to maintain a fading regal splendour. There, in misery and depression, he died fifty years later.

For eight years Bobbing John faithfully served James, and entered with zest into the whole political game. In the interests of his master, he engineered the Spanish invasion of Scotland by Cardinal Alberoni, and in order to cover the king's visit to Spain he went to Voghera, where he was arrested and imprisoned. The invasion was abortive, and Mar planned the next move of marrying Clementina, a Sobieski of Poland, to the lonely exiled king. In 1722 another rising was planned, and Mar was actually authorised by the king to call a new Parliament of Scotland, but the attempt never materialised. By this time the shrewd earl saw that the Stuart cause was lost and the only ally left was the Vatican. It was time for him to quit the royal service. So with his master's sanction he crossed to Geneva, where, once more, he was imprisoned. Only the energetic pressure of his old friend Stair secured his release, who added to his purchase over Mar by securing him the offer of a government pension—on terms! It has never been proved that he accepted this pension from the British government, although both James and his adherents disowned Mar after this. Nor was Mar sorry at leaving James, for had he not assured Sir John Erskine, " We are going on in our old dull way, one day being as like another as two eggs, and those eaten without pepper and salt " ? He returned for a time to Paris and Clichy and finally settled at Aix-la-Chapelle, where he had the joy of the company of his son, Lord Thomas Erskine, for certain holiday seasons. Indeed, it is through this son Thomas that we have the choicest and most fascinating pieces of Mar's writing.

In the leisure of his retirement this wise and experienced man of the world, who himself had seen such changes, placed on paper for the guidance of his son his potted philosophy. Already, while still in the thick of politics in 1708, he had mused, " It is a wonder to see how this world does go," and again in 1715 as he waited for the clansmen to gather at Braemar, he scribbled out his thoughts for his son, lest he should die in the forthcoming campaign. Indeed, later he had the temerity to refer to those as " idle hours." Idle hours, indeed, preparing for a national rising ! But it was really in France he set down to the task. His nephew, young Paterson of Bannockburn, wrote out a copy of them for wider use. Earl John had the fine literary flair, for he said, " I have endorsed them—not improperly, I hope—JEWELS OF SCOTLAND."

Part of Mar's so-called " Legacy " was directed to Lord Thomas Erskine, who, by the way, had been trained in the French service as a soldier. This contains much shrewd wisdom for the guidance of his heir, touching on his character and conduct. He has a word on life's ideals.

" Let your chief care and study ever be how you can be most serviceable in the station in which Providence places you, to God in the first place, to your country in the next, and consequently to your king . . . You have such principles already that I hope honesty in all your ways and doings will be natural to you. Do not neglect acquiring riches, when you have becoming opportunities, but let not that be your chief view and aim, and endeavour to be more good than rich."

Here the astute and clever old diplomat drops all the tricks and politics and speaks out frankly like a godly preacher. Nor indeed does he forget to guide Thomas in ecclesiastical matters, as when he says :—

" I had the service of the Church of England set up at Alloa, for which I made a chapel, it being nearest my way of thinking in those matters, a medium betwixt the bare, unbecoming nakedness of the Presbyterian service in Scotland, and the gaudy, affected and ostentive way of the Church of Rome."

But he becomes even more personal than this, for he laid down rules for Thomas in his choice of a wife !

" Take care you marry not for love alone ; that soon goes off where there is not a foundation of other qualities to support it, but be sure that you do not marry, where you cannot love . . . Avoid a disagreeable woman."

This last advice gets point from the extraordinarily disagreeable wife that his brother James had chosen, an ungovernable creature whom Grange sent off to St. Kilda. But who is to know beforehand how a wife will turn out ? There's the rub ! And so he concludes,

" After all your care in the choice of a wife . . . your happening will depend on God."

Here, surely, all wisdom ends, and here Thomas began, for he wisely chose Lady Charlotte Hope, a fine and generous-hearted woman, who inherited a fine tradition of public service and private probity and honour.

Mar had built up the family fortune, like a skilful architect, and then he lost it. Grange retrieved the confiscated estate of Alloa—the Aberdeen estate went for good—and he linch-pinned the family future by marrying his son to Mar's daughter, and so retaining the land in the Erskine connection. But Earl John started his castle-building again, even in exile :—

> " If ever you come to be rich enough to increase the estate, it will be your interest and that of the family to purchase near to Alloa than anywhere else, and the nearer it be still the better. The estate of Clackmannan, which joins it, would be the most convenient purchase you can make."

He had not forgotten that Bruce of Clackmannan had gone bankrupt and the estate was being sold up. But he forgot that the Erskines were mighty lucky to have even Alloa in that their evil day.

With a warning to Thomas not to fall into bookish ways and become a stuffy scholar moping around the library, he urges him to enjoy the sports of the field, and to take walking exercise. These, he assured his son, would be much more beneficial for his health than taking bottles of medicine. And the old philosopher was right. We can see him shake his head, with the old bobbing motion, as he confesses he is too old to learn the game of cards ; enough for him that he over-indulged a passion for dice and hazard.

But Mar was a thinker, as well as a visionary. He loved his native Scotland and he wanted to see her great and free. With all an exile's passionate devotion, he started building his ideal Scotland, and he allowed his pen to run on, as he re-made his broken and betrayed but still beloved land. Of James he could write : " I heartily forgive him all the unjust and unmerited treatment I have met from him . . . he has been an unlucky man from his cradle," but this never shook his stout faith that Scotland should be separate from England and should have a Parliament of its own. " I hope the time will still come," he wrote, " that there will be a Scots Parliament on this bottom." He saw clearly too that London planned the extermination of the clan system in the Highlands, but he countered this with : " Clanship in our country is what ought to be encouraged and kept up as much as possible." The Parliament, too, should be elected every seven years and be compelled to meet at least every two years. The link with England should be as slight as possible, but the alliance with Ireland should be strengthened and the two nations that have so much in common in blood and tradition should be " knit well together." He went further and higher in his flight of fancy, when he outlined a scheme of military alliance between Ireland, Scotland and France, whereby a force of 10,000 soldiers from Ireland and Scotland should be trained in France, and 10,000 French soldiers should be trained in these two countries. This force could be increased to 40,000 in times of emergency and would provide an irresistible army to maintain peace. In November, 1727, Mar went even further than this, and reviving a scheme which had been sponsored by the King of Sweden just at the time when he was accidentally killed, he proposed to the Duke of Orleans that George I should rule over England and the East and West Indies, while Scotland, Ireland and part of the American Plantations should constitute a quite separate and independent confederacy. It seemed a fair divide! And to the visionary, how easy and how promising!

But Earl John could come down to solid earth. He did not disdain to deal with Scotland as she was. In fact, the exile saw more than the worthy bailie who strutted up the Edinburgh High Street, for he saw the old Palace of Holyrood, not in its shabby and melancholy ruins, but rebuilt and restored to its former grandeur, and his architect's eye glistened with joy at the vision. Earl John was the man who stirred in the somnolent city minds the passion to preserve the disappearing pile. And if we pride ourselves, as we rightly do, in our royal palace, should we not acknowledge our debt to the versatile and accomplished Mar of the Rising?

But he saw in his exile's vision more than the old Palace. He saw the crushed and cramped metropolis on the Castle Hill overflowing into a lovely, widespread and prosperous capital. Notice what he writes:—

"The Metropolis (Edinburgh) is in an inconvenient situation, but could be improved by making a large bridge of three stories of arches over the low ground betwixt the Norloch and the Physick Garden from the High Street at Halkerston's Wynd to the Moultrie Hill, where there might be many fine streets built, as the inhabitants increased, the access to them being easy on all hands . . . One large and long street in a straight line, where the long gate is now, on one side of it would be a fine opportunity for gardens down to the Norloch, and on the other side towards Broughton. By selling the places on the end of the bridge for houses and the vaults or arches below for warehouses and cellars, the charge of the bridge might be near defrayed."

Here, indeed, we have the origin of the glorious Princes

E

Street, with its lovely gardens, the joy and pride of the capital. Truly, Earl John was a man of many parts, and if as the adventurer of the 'Fifteen he still rouses to fury the perfervid Jacobite for his incompetence at Sheriff-muir, may he not re-establish his claim on Scottish hearts by so happy a vision of the Scotland that is to be? That he was wise and shrewd as a statesman is patent for all to see, but it is not so generally recognised that he was a visionary with a fertile mind.

Nor did this exhaust the fertility of that versatile mind. He saw beyond Edinburgh to the wide promising plains of the Lowlands, and a glance at the map showed him that it was not such a far cry from the upper reaches of the Forth to those of the Clyde. He hit upon the idea that these two mighty estuaries could with little trouble and expense be united, so avoiding the long and stormy voyage round the northern firths. With Olympian grandeur, he hands out to his countrymen this fruitful idea in these words :—

> "The making a canal betwixt the Rivers Forth and Clyde would be a great improvement to Scotland, as well as of great service to the trade of the whole island, especially the Indian trade by saving a dangerous, long passage round Britain, since by that canal the west and east sea would be joined. The way for leading this canal is from near Glasgow by Kilsyth to the mouth of the river Carron, below Falkirk. It is computed that thirty thousand pounds sterling might do the work, but should it cost the double, it would be well bestowed, and be soon repaid, the profit arising from the canal, if there were any trade in the country.
>
> "There might also be a good road made, for transporting merchandise by land betwixt Glasgow

on the Clyde and the Forth, by Takmedoon, St.
Ninians and the Throsk, where large barks can come
up the Forth, and great ships to Alloa, which is but
three miles lower . . . The merchants might have
warehouses at Throsk for their goods, and from
thence it is easy bringing them by water to Alloa,
whereby they could be shift for Edinburgh, London,
etc."

Here, without doubt, we have the germ-thought,
the almost prophetic vision that foresaw the Forth and
Clyde canal. It was delayed until after the 'Forty-Five,
and by a strange irony, it was the monies got from the
sale of the Jacobite estates that provided the capital for
the enterprise. Perhaps Earl John, sitting at his writing
desk at Aix-la-Chapelle with the evening shadows of
life gathering round him and peering into the future,
would not have had it otherwise. He certainly by that
time knew better than look to London for the needed
money.

And so the flair of the architect was there to the last.

Disowned by his Stuart king, ousted by Hay and " that
firebrand of a bishop " Attebury, sick and disillusioned by
the whole trickery of politics, John Erskine clung des-
perately to his bright pavilions. His love for Scotland
was so great and intense that when his hand could not
guide any longer the plunging ship of State, he still went on
building his gorgeous castles in the air, and planning a
brighter and happier land.

Take him for all in all, John, the sixth Earl of Mar,
was a remarkable man. He has stamped his name in-
effaceably on Scottish history. Most writers have villified
and decried him for his one weak hour at Sheriffmuir and
have ignored his years of splendid achievement. Men
use three means to influence their fellows, the sword, the

tongue and the pen. This great Scotsman may have failed in generalship, but his persuasive tongue converted his great ideal of Union into a living and fruitful reality, and his pen, which he knew to be more powerful than his sword, produced for Scotland jewels whose wealth is still untold. As a young man he saw his vision, and, unlike most of us, he translated it into fact. As an old man he dreamed his dream. From both alike his long-lost land has derived immeasurable good. Did Macaulay tell his thoughts in exile, when he wrote :—

> " To my true king I offered free from stain,
>   Courage and faith ; vain faith and courage vain.
> For him, I threw lands, honours, wealth away,
>   And one dear hope, that was more prized than
>   they " ?

BIBLIOGRAPHY

A journal of the Earl of Mar's proceedings. 1716.

The Earl of Mar's legacies to Scotland and to his son, Lord Erskine, 1722-1727. Ed. Hon. Stuart Erskine. 1897. Scottish History Society, vol. 26.

The Mar and Kellie Papers. 2 vols. 1904. Historical MSS. Commission.

ALEXANDER, Lord LINDSAY—
   The Earldom of Mar. 2 vols. 1882.

ALISTAIR and HENRIETTA TAYLER—
   1715 : the story of the rising. 1936.

CHAPTER III

SIR RALPH ABERCROMBY OF TULLIBODY

THE sands of Egypt formed the stage for Montgomery's crucial battle of Alamein in 1942; they saw also Abercromby triumph at Aboukir in 1801. Both battles turned the tide for Britain in a European conflict, the one against Napoleon and the other against Hitler, and although the battles were pitched far away from the central theatres, they marked in each case the approaching doom of a continental dictator. True, it was the end of Abercromby's chequered career, as it was but the beginning of Montgomery's brilliant generalship, but Alexandria was the prize in both cases; its gain or loss decided the final issue. And by a perverse fate the situations were entirely reversed. It was the gain of Alexandria through Abercromby's victory that foiled Buonaparte. It was because Montgomery succeeded where the French had failed, that Rommel was sent running to the West. And still another irony lies in the tactics of the battles. For the French general in 1801 used the same feint manœuvre on the one flank while driving for a break through on the coast, but he failed in this the very strategy that crowned Montgomery with glory.

And so the comparison might go on . . .

Much is known and more will yet be told of the hero of Alamein, but of Abercromby of Aboukir the common man takes little heed. And this is strange. In his day was he not the outstanding general? Did not London go delirious over his victories of the Helder and present him with a golden sword? Did he not die in the very time of victory and pass like Nelson into unclouded immortality ? Indeed, he did, and justice demands that his name and fame be ever fresh in the hearts of his compatriots.

He was born in the smallest county of Great Britain, the tiny area named on the map, Clackmannan. In October, 1734, he opened his eyes as a new-born babe in the family house in the village of Menstrie. This house, however, was a mere appendage to the property of Tullibody, where in fact Ralph was reared. Tullibody House was and is a plain, solid, typically Scots baronial mansion, lying a mile to the west of Alloa and close by the placid waters of the Forth. Fishing was good and Ralph was fond of it. His father, George Abercromby, was by profession a lawyer and had in fact been called to the bar, but he never practised. His knowledge of law was so sound and his grasp so complete that he was appointed to lecture on Civil Law in Edinburgh University, during a brief absence of Professor Dundas. Besides being, as we shall see, a very wise father, he was also a man of learning and he arranged for such a classical education for Ralph that right to the end of his life the soldier took delight in the pages of Cicero and Horace, of Tacitus and Livy. The basis for this cultural education was made by James Syme, a private tutor engaged by his father. Syme was a gifted graduate who gave much more than Latin and Greek to Ralph. In the schoolroom at Tullibody House the boy imbibed the virtues of self-discipline and moral rectitude that formed the framework of a splendid character. He got from Syme also a passion for justice and a hatred for all forms of oppression. This underlying sympathy with the down-trodden predisposed him towards, first, the Americans in their struggle for independence, then to the French Revolutionaries and, finally, to the abused and maltreated Irish peasantry. And yet, withal, Syme was a likeable and gentle creature. When he had taught Ralph for some years, the boy passed on for a short time to the select school of Mr. Moir in Alloa. The strong Mar influence gave this school a distinct Jacobite flavour, and caused the pupils to be somewhat suspect to the government, but Ralph was quite impervious to the political tenets of Mr. Moir,[1] and his schoolfellow, Lord Elgin, was later to co-operate in the expedition to Aboukir. But Syme was the favourite of the Abercrombys, and when the parish was looking for a minister in 1750 their influence secured the place for him. This was, unfortunately for Syme, the signal for troubles. The colliers of Alloa were keen on another preacher, John Skirven, and when baulked of their choice they turned against all authority. Alexander and George Abercromby arrived with the Gargunnock minister to serve the edict for Syme, and were so maltreated that they were glad to retreat to Tullibody House, while the colliers seized the kirk, rang the bell defiantly and hung a flag of victory from the steeple. But the victory was short-lived. In November, four companies of soldiers arrived in the town and the minister was ordained without opposition. Ralph, now a scholar of Rugby, must have read with relish the letters of his father, describing the settlement of his old tutor.

In 1752 Ralph left Rugby and returned to his father's country home. The handsome, charming boy, now polished in his manners, called doubtless at the old Manse to have a cheery word with his old tutor, but he could notice the declining strength of the cleric, and when next winter he was attending the law classes in Edinburgh

[1]Jacobites escaping from the Battle of Falkirk in 1746 were caught and wiped out near Tullibody House. This would be enough to banish Jacobitism from his head.

University, he was not surprised to learn that James **Syme**
was dead. But life—and his father—drove Ralph on.
He took the classes of Moral and Natural Philosophy and
of Civil Law, and although never brilliant he was a keen
student, an urbane and prepossessing comrade, and a
fellow of sound sense. The other students learned
to trust his judgment and came to hold him in real affection. The wide sweep of his mind and the mass of his
intellect appealed to their developing powers.

But Edinburgh was not enough for a youth with
reach and promise. His father sent him to Leipzig to
round off his studies with a course in Civil Law. This
would give the hall-mark to the successful man of law.
So off he posted to Holland en route for Germany, and had
for company Lord Elgin his old schoolmate, who was
making for an Academy in Paris. Sir James Yorke, our
Minister there, smilingly charged them with a Jacobite
schooling, for he knew that the unfortunate Prince Charles
had still his contacts in Scotland. The Leipzig spell
broadened and deepened his knowledge not only of law
but of Germany and the whole political set-up of the
Continent. He watched the achievements and talents of
Frederick the Great, he studied his military tactics and he
was filled with admiration for such a successful leader.
He saw also the value of such an ally in the coming clash
with France. Home he came, but not to be a lawyer, no
matter how urbane and fashionable. He broke the news
to his father that his heart lay in soldiering, and—to the
honour of wise old George—it did not break the paternal
heart! By March, 1756, it was clear there was nothing
else to be done, and so he bought a cornetcy for Ralph
in the Third Dragoon Guards. The lad was in time—
just in time—for the decisive Seven Years War. It
remains an astonishing fact that the officer who served

the Protestant cause in Hanover in 1758 was also the head and front of our offensive against Napoleon in 1801.

Well, to Germany he went, after two years of training at home, and there he studied at close quarters the discipline and technique of the Prussian military machine. He loved freedom of conscience too much ever to be a convert to its spirit, but he was wise enough to abstract from it the best in its methods. And these were two: firstly, to maintain discipline, secondly, to safeguard the health of the common soldier. These studies in soldiering he prosecuted privately, and on his own initiative, for the morale of the British troops was so low that few officers were sufficiently interested to bother about such matters. This flair, together with his broad intellectual background, singled out Ralph as a desirable aide-de-camp for Sir William Pitt in 1758, and henceforth he stepped up the well-marked ladder of military promotion. His father bought a troop for him in 1762, thus making him a captain, and after a period of service in Ireland, which opened his eyes to the brutal rule of the English landed gentry there, he was promoted major in 1770, lieutenant-colonel in 1773, brevet-colonel in 1780, and from 1781 to 1783, he commanded the 103rd King's Irish Infantry until it was disbanded in 1783, when he was retired on half-pay. Like Nelson himself, it seemed he was of no more use to his country. The navy, like the army, was reduced to vanishing point. The age-old delusion was potent then as in 1935, that we can be a safe and strong people with a small navy and a smaller army.

It is in this period that the personal character and convictions of Ralph Abercromby come into prominence. There have always been soldiers who ignored both politics and morals, simply carrying out their military duties with no thought of the rights and wrongs of the larger national issues.

> Theirs not to reason why,
> Theirs but to do and die . . .

But Abercromby was not made and not educated in this mould. He read, studied and thought far beyond the narrow horizons of the old professional soldier. For long he had admired from afar the sterling qualities of Washington, and when the foolhardy policy of Lord North drove the colonists to arms, he and many others had too much sympathy with them to serve against them. Lord Effingham voiced Ralph's feelings, when he wrote, " I cannot without reproach from my own conscience, consent to bear arms against my fellow-subjects in America, in what, to my discernment, is not a clear cause." It was in no party spirit he so acted, but from a broad and humanitarian principle. He just refused to take part in what was after all a civil war within the same state.

This deep humanitarian compassion explains his reluctance to assail the legitimate claims of the French Revolutionaries. He sympathised with their sufferings and constantly advocated mediation in the growing differences between them and the monarchy of England. Indeed, it was only when they unguardedly declared war on these islands, that he threw himself keenly into the struggle as into a crusade for freedom. The same compassion shewed itself later in his efforts to bring peace to Ireland, as we shall see.

Meanwhile, his retirement was not idle. He loved the house at Tullibody, now dearer than ever to him since his mother died in 1767. She had filled an honoured place in the community for many years. Had she not joined with Lady Frances Erskine and Lady Cathcart in supporting the young artist, David Allan of Alloa, at the St. Luke's Academy at Rome ? True, she did not live to know of his world success in 1773 in gaining the

gold medal for his masterpiece, " The Origin of Painting,"
but she was a lady of a kind heart and a generous hand.
Nor did Sir Ralph lose contact with Allan. In the year
in which he had lost his mother he gained a wife, Anne
Menzies of Fernton, who loyally presented him in succession with four devoted and able sons. When the
third son, James, was a child of two, probably about
1775, Allan, newly home from Rome, insisted on repaying
his old debt to the house, by executing an oil painting of
the beautiful child. For long the picture adorned the
walls of Tullibody House, a tribute alike to mother, son,
grandson and artist.

Local matters were not beneath his notice. How
could they be, when both his parents had shown so good
an example ? " Auld Tullibody," as his honoured father
had been called by his tenants, was a worthy elder in the
united parishes of Alloa and Tullibody, and had he not in
1760 re-roofed the historic old church of Tullibody with
blue tiles ? He even adorned the bare churchyard with a
few trees, and thought he had improved its aspect. Not
so thought Robert Mason, the gravedigger, for he promptly
pulled the trees from the sacred earth. They were planted
again and uprooted also again. So the laird planted the
gravedigger into Clackmannan gaol ! And planted in
a sense he was, for he refused to leave the unsavoury gaol
until he knew his crime. And " Tullibody," the erst-
while professor of Civil Law, was hard put to justifying
his action. Mason's father lay beneath these trees, but
how could he rise at Judgment Day ? The laird must
promise to be there in such an hour to axe the offending
tree ! But neither laird nor cotter could give such promise.
So the trees were finally transplanted outside the churchyard wall, and the local incident was over. And Ralph
improved upon his father, for he secured a bell to call the

faithful to worship. It was none the worse of being a ship's bell. It came from a man-of-war and bore the inscription, " Duke of Kingston, 1756." Right on until 1837 it merrily called the people to peace and not to war.

It gladdened the old laird's heart to see his two promising sons made, like himself, honoured elders of the Church, for the Session Minute of the 5th July, 1768, states :—

> " Captain Ralph Abercromby, younger, of Tulli-
> body, and Alexander Abercromby, Esq., advocate,
> were this day ordained elders ; in consequence of
> the edict being served, and no objections offered,
> they received the right hand of fellowship and took
> their seats in the Session."

Ralph was now married and settled in Tullibody House, while his father, having acquired Brucefield House, moved out there and functioned as laird and elder in the parish of Clackmannan. But the beautiful epilogue was still to come, for he spent his last days in Ralph's town house in Edinburgh, respected and loved for his wisdom and his wit, and when these days closed in 1800, his brilliant son's had but a year to run. Meanwhile Ralph sponsored a school in the village of Tullibody for the encouragement of reading, and with others he graciously dispensed the Poor Funds to the needy and the destitute. A man of wide culture himself, he sought to imbue a love of it in all ranks of the community.

This led him into troubles. In a weak moment he was inveigled into politics, and politics then were both bitter and corrupt. He allowed himself to be chosen for Parliament in 1773, but it was a venomous campaign. Colonel Erskine, kinsman of the Mars, was a dangerous foe, and in a pamphlet had impugned the character of Lord Kennet, an honoured member of the College of

Justice. So Ralph, the soldier, threw down the gage, for Kennet was precluded from self-defence. The duel was arranged. The spot was chosen. The contestants appeared with their seconds. The pistols were primed. The shots were fired—harmlessly! The seconds agreed to stop the fight. The exciting moment was over. Not so the chagrin and the spite, for Ralph despised and never quite forgave the vile aspersion on his friend.

But this was just the start. Soon Ralph found that matters were corrupt inside as well as outside Westminster. If Sir Lawrence Dundas had backed him, he expected him to do his bidding. Why not? And if not, well—he would put him out. It was all so simple! But the lawyer-soldier did not see it that way, and Dundas found he had backed a loser. Ralph was not made to do another's bidding. His own mind and heart were big enough to guide him aright. If this were politics, far better to live a quiet life. And so he did. He refused to be re-elected in 1788, and when in 1797 he was thrust again unwillingly into Parliament, he promptly resigned. Politics, to him, were a dirty game, and he left it to the jobbers and the trimmers.

Indeed, more immediate matters concerned him. At Tullibody he supervised the education of his boys, but now they were ready for college, and must follow their father's footsteps. So he took house in the capital and set himself the joy and duty of seeing them through college. In this he revelled. He was freed for some years from military duties, for remembering his attitude in the American War the government had no use for his services now. Like Nelson, he was now a useless and forgotten supernumerary. It suited Ralph. He lived again in the spirit and literature of the Classics, and drew around his dinner table a small but select circle of intimates.

And was he not the perfect host ?   Amply erudite himself in many spheres of knowledge, he yet contrived to lead the talk to the favourite theme of his guest, so gaining more knowledge for himself and giving delight to his friend. He even found time to hear the popular lectures of Dr. Hardy on Church History. And happy for him to be in the Edinburgh of the Scots Renaissance ! In one day he might see in the High Street such giants as Hume, Robertson, Ferguson, Burns and Monboddo.

And so his life might easily have flowed on in cultured ease.

Such was not to be . . .

It is a cruel fate that gives a soldier an independent mind, and such was the mind of Ralph Abercromby. Already he had given proof of his stout convictions in refusing to fight against George Washington, and the wiseheads at the War Office—for all their racketeering— had logic enough to dislike him. They saw like other officials that no army can function if its commanders pick and choose their causes. But the retired colonel was a man of sense and he hoped that the triumphant success of American democracy would engender wider freedom throughout the world. He was no bigoted reactionary against the flaming pages of Tom Paine, and when the fury of the French Revolution broke upon Europe, he showed towards it a cautious and discriminating approval.   How it shocked the violent reactionaries ! His mildest judgments they took and twisted and exaggerated.   And it was when an infuriated gentry proposed the most brutal and insensate methods of political repression in Britain that this thinking soldier offered wiser guidance. He held that fetters and firelocks can never chain or kill opinions and ideas. Only a better and truer opinion can kill a false one. Knowledge of truth

alone can destroy error. And so he launched a crusade
to give more and better knowledge to the rank and file of
the people, and Edinburgh knew him at this time for
something of an apostle. But he went even farther than
this. A member of the peerage had been so rash as to
approve of the French experiment, only to find that his
old Edinburgh associates cut him in the High Street and
carefully avoided his hospitality. It was then that Ralph,
with studied timeliness, offered the noble lord his hand
and heart. Young Lord Daer was another firebrand,
who, round the generous dinner-table of the Abercrombys,
warmed up to his schemes of social reform. And how
the enlightened colonel glowed as he saw the clean and
honest passions of youth! He often said that if a man
were not a rebel at twenty he would be base at forty.

These were remarkable sentiments for a colonel,
even for a retired colonel. And he genuinely believed
them. But Wordsworth was not the only keen mind
that became slowly disillusioned with the French political
venture, for while Ralph hoped against hope that dis-
cussion would clear the air between the Revolutionaries
and the policy of Pitt, he saw that liberty had gone to the
heads of the French. They needed a Frederick to hold
them in check, and no Frederick was in sight.

In a single day the whole picture changed. France
declared war on England on the 1st of February, 1793.
The defences on this island were at their very lowest. Both
army and navy were totally unfit to face the political
enthusiasts of France. Once again, and not for the last
time, Britain was caught quite unprepared for a mortal
struggle. Colonel A. la Court might have been writing of
1939 instead of 1793 when he said :—

" It is true that this great war was ultimately
successful . . . but this result must not blind us to

the fact that neither statesmen nor Parliament had foreseen the gathering storm, nor had they taken any precautions to weather it . . . no less than eight years passed before England was able to strike firm blows with her army, and fifteen years before the weapon was so tempered that it could seriously influence the course of military events. During this period how many hundred thousand lives were lost, and how many millions poured out in that gigantic struggle ! . . ."

And even more pertinently he follows this with :—

"It is not too much to say that had England, at the outset of the war, been able to place in the field an army equal in numbers to that with which, two hundred years before, Elizabeth had confronted Philip of Spain, the great war would have been strangled at its birth. Then the world would have been spared the frightful losses and huge weight of debt which still hamper the physical development and embarrass the finances of the nations of Europe."

And some say that history does not repeat itself !

The effect of French rashness was immediate. Ralph Abercromby swung into line as a loyal soldier in a single night and next morning had dashed off a note to Whitehall, asking to serve in the national peril. And, still more wonderful to tell, Whitehall forgot the past and made him a major-general with a brigade to command. (*Dictionary of National Biography* gives 1787 as date of promotion to major-general but Col. A. la Court gives the more likely date, *i.e.*, 1793.) By the 21st March, he had embarked at Leith for Antwerp with his entire brigade. But what a brigade ! Even Sir Henry Calvert had to admit that Abercromby's lot were a mere mob of old men and weak boys, like Falstaff's ragged ruffians. Two of the three

SIR RALPH ABERCROMBY
(Scottish National Portrait Gallery).
By kind permission

battalions were so weak and short as to be counted *hors de combat*. And note that fateful date, the 21st of March. It was the very day, eight years later, when Ralph was to receive his death wound at Aboukir.

Nothing is more exasperating than the details of a campaign. Far be it from us to dive into the tiresome minutiae of positions and movements by which Abercromby showed his gifts as a great commander in the field. It is better, once the broad issues are made clear, to see the highlights of a career that closed in such spectacular glory. But after careful study of his four fighting expeditions, it is clear beyond doubt that Ralph Abercromby was a soldier whose fate was to be matched against the almost impossible. He was given forces which in each case were quite undisciplined, and completely lacked *esprit de corps*. The equipment was both out of date and inadequate. Worse still, he was given tasks of such difficulty as only a dull and stupid Cabinet could have proposed. Repeatedly he had to carry through combined operations by land and sea, as at the Helder and Aboukir, which called for generalship of the highest order. And more than generalship he showed. His courage even in the thick of the fight rose conspicuously with danger. He seemed to scent a battle, like a noble horse, and his officers were hard put to it to keep him at the point of central command. The grave lawyer and scholar slipped into the background and he turned into the dashing and impetuous commander. Those were days when high command did not imply immunity from wounds. G.H.Q. seemed to be anywhere in the field where the C.-in-C. happened to be standing! It was this spirited leadership that quickly won the utter devotion of the raw recruits and it made them do deeds that surprised themselves. His soldiers saw him being wounded at Nimeguen

F

in the first campaign of 1794, as later they were to watch
two horses being shot under him in the thick of the fray
at Egmont. It made them think again about what an
officer was. The old contempt gave place to a new manly
devotion.

And besides this personal equation, Ralph applied
two excellent principles of war. A man with a powerful
weapon in his hand, even though he be in uniform, tends
to be reckless and irresponsible. But Ralph soon made
his soldiers feel that they were under authority. For
reckless behaviour they would surely be brought to book.
Slowly and steadily this sense of discipline permeated all
ranks. His soldiers became an army. His second principle was no less vital. The health of the soldier had with
him first priority. He cared as no other commander of
his day for the well-being of the trudging infantryman.
When he lay adying at Aboukir, some kind officer brought
a soldier's blanket and placed it beneath his head to afford
him some relief. But Abercromby was most insistent
that the blanket should be returned to the soldier, for,
said he, " a soldier's blanket is of great consequence."
This concern of the general for the common soldier was
characteristic of the man.

Britain has the uncanny and unpredictable knack
of producing in danger's hour the very man to meet
the situation. It was so with Raleigh, with Nelson, with
Lloyd George and Churchill. Not less true was it in
the case of Ralph Abercromby. With all due respect to
the fine qualities of the Duke of York, it was undoubtedly
the laird of Tullibody who shone out in the first phase of
the Napoleonic War as the most brilliant commander in
the field. In the first disastrous moves of 1794 and 1795
his was the one lonely success among a humiliating series
of defeats. Did he not at Cateau capture the French

general Chapuy himself, besides thirty-five pieces of
cannon ? Less conspicuously but just as brilliantly
he saved the retreating remnants of his army, as it wilted
under the sledge-hammer blows of the trained Frenchman.
And nature was arrayed against him, too, for as the campaign dragged on into the winter months, drifts of snow
and sheets of sleet disintegrated the troops, so that even
roll-calls were abandoned. One witness described a
mother dying in the very act of suckling her child, and
the dead child with the milk frozen on its very lip. The
long and tedious retreat to Bremen halved the British
forces, and it was only Abercromby's generalship that
saved the other half.

One patent fact in this his first command is the
loyalty and co-operation of his brother generals. Dundas
and Cathcart—after all, near neighbours in Clackmannan
county—ably strengthened his hands day after day,
and it would be surprising if on the bloody fields of Flanders
they were not united by the same vision of the green
shoulders of the Ochils. But it was the same with Abercromby all through to the end. He could make deep
and lasting friendships with brothers in arms, but with
the dabbling, double-crossing politicians he could do
nothing but quarrel. The Duke of York, General Coote,
and above all the immortal Sir John Moore, were all his
constant and admiring friends. It was, as it ever has
been in British history, that the soldiers were better men
than the statesmen that ruled them. Ere this study be
over the devotion of Sir John Moore will shine out as a
star in Abercromby's blackest night.

Out of the ill-conceived adventure he alone emerged
with conspicuous honour. He returned to England
to find his name was on nearly every lip, and the king
honoured him without delay by making him a Knight of

the Bath.   It is true, as one writer puts its, that no one was more surprised than himself when he was counted his country's greatest general.   How like him! He took these gaudy things with philosophic calm, and he showed some spirit in the matter only when they went too far.   To the powers at Whitehall the Flanders fiasco yielded but one crumb of comfort : they had found a real commander.

And they needed him.   For the French with typical revolutionary fervour had made no little trouble in the West Indies.   Not content with smashing the British arms in Flanders, they dealt shrewd and costly blows at Guadeloupe, St. Lucia, St. Vincent, Grenada and Marie Galante.   These they not only seized but devastated to the tune of some £72 millions.   It could not go on. Sir Ralph was given sole command of the 15,000 fighting men, and sailed from Spithead in the foulest weather. The flagship *Glory*, with Admiral Christian and the Commander-in-Chief aboard, belied its name in such tempestuous seas, and has interest only in showing the imperturbable spirit of the leader.   It is related that in the height of the storm his personal servant rushed into the cabin, where he and the admiral were conferring, with the breathless announcement : " We are going to be drowned."   " Very well," replied Sir Ralph, " you go to bed."   But the storm was not to be so easily disposed of as the servant, and twice the ships had to return to port.   It was March, 1796, before the operations were under way in the West Indies, however, and soon it became clear that Abercromby had bred men like himself, for Sir John Moore emerges now as a commander of the same bold and splendid calibre as his superior.   Moore's brilliant dash against St. Lucia was followed by a succession of capitulations by French and Dutch garrisons and the destruction of the enemy fleet at Port of Spain.   The diary of Moore presents many illuminating sidelights on the behaviour of the army commander. While at St. Lucia he wrote :—

> " Sir Ralph came here yesterday morning . . . (He) is very short-sighted. Without a glass he sees nothing, but with it he observes ground quickly and well. He has the zeal and eagerness of youth, and for his age has much activity both of mind and body . . ."

He was not so flattering later, when Abercromby came storming down on his dispositions ; then, he was " blind " and " out of humour," and when Moore was left almost alone as Governor his pen ran venomous ink. " The General and Admiral think they have cleared themselves from all trouble by running away from it. They have, however, hurt their character as military men." Moore, was, as a matter of fact, very peeved because he was being left behind on the island, while his commander was returning to England. He confessed he " would give the world to get home." No wonder he vented his chagrin by noting, " I was infinitely disappointed at not seeing Sir Ralph, and I cannot but think him most inexcusable . . ." He went even further and confided to his diary, " I am extremely dissatisfied with Sir Ralph, whom I believe to be a worthy but a weak man." But these outpourings were not the real Moore, for in his calmer moments he admitted, " The kind and friendly manner in which Sir Ralph has uniformly behaved to me . . . is such that . . . I know no person to whom I am so much obliged." The foundations were now being laid for a comradeship that lasted till death.

The main task of the expeditionary force in the West Indies was now accomplished and Abercromby was recalled. Soldiers of his calibre were needed nearer home, for Napoleon was stirring up trouble in Ireland. Augustine Birrell used to say that it was the land where the inevitable never happened and the impossible always happened. When the victor of St. Lucia went there in December, 1797, he was faced with the impossible. His keen sense of justice roused him to feel for a downtrodden people, like Newbolt later,

" Long ago that anguish took thee,
    Ireland, Ireland, green and fair,
  Spoilers strong in darkness took thee,
    Broke thy heart and left thee there."

Already, as a young subaltern, he had met and loved the native Irish. He knew them for a high-spirited people, and if they were bitter and disaffected towards England, the blame lay, he was convinced, with the English themselves and their misgovernment. He little knew that in being appointed as Commander-in-Chief there, he was merely the political pawn of Lord Camden, who spoke him fair while he double-crossed him. Reams could be written of the complicated situation at this time. Suffice it to say that the gentry and landowners, most of whom were magistrates, failed to apply the restraints of civil law and called in the soldiers to plot the whole country in small groups and harass the people into trembling submission. But the people secured arms and so a civil strife became a civil war. The soldiers got out of hand, being thus left in virtual command of the country. It was the policy of the new Commander to make the soldiers feel the firm hand of discipline upon them, and this he achieved by strict orders and solemn warnings. He invited the peasants to hand in their stolen arms. But when the Commander-in-Chief urged the civil magistrates to do their duty first, before calling in the soldier, all the intrigue of Dublin combined to frustrate him. The Lord-Lieutenant was courteous but spineless. The gentry framed up an imputation of political manœuvring against Sir Ralph, from which Camden completely absolved him. The mud, however, had been thrown. " No man," said Abercromby to Camden, " can be indifferent to his own character," and therewith he asked to be relieved of his impossible post. In leaving his command after only five months, the distinguished soldier knew very well that if he had disturbed the cruel snobbery of the Irish gentry, he had earned the admiration of both the Duke of York and His Majesty the King. He was at once offered and accepted the Scottish Command, and so came home for a short time to his own friends and surroundings.

Once again he had emerged from a forbidding task with his honour unstained and his prestige unimpaired.

He was fated to enjoy the comforts of his native land for but a short time. The Cabinet considered this a timely moment for an attack on Holland. And so it was. Napoleon was tied up in Egypt. The navy had steadily risen in strength in six years to 507 ships with 120,000 sailors and marines. The Allies had scored successes against the French on the Rhine, in Switzerland and in Italy. Furthermore, Russia now offered help in the shape of thousands of wild, unruly soldiers. The aim of the British was to capture what remained of the Dutch fleet after Camperdown ; the aim of the Russians to ease the advance of Suvarov. To the world it was announced as the restoration of the House of Orange to rule Holland, but this was mere bluff.

So Abercromby was appointed to command the expedition, with John Moore as his right arm. Fortescue compares them to Stonewall Jackson and Lee. Already in his sixty-fifth year and enjoying the sweet joys of his delightful home in Edinburgh, Sir Ralph at once tore himself away from his devoted wife and posted south to Kent where a ragged and nondescript army was put in training. It was really a desperate adventure. The heads round the Cabinet table little dreamed how delicate and daring such a combined operation must be. Even with seasoned warriors it was a gamble, but with the raw reservists now called up it was a forlorn hope. Nor had Sir Ralph any illusions about success. His letters to his wife make it plain that he disliked the ill-conceived campaign. But on he went with his plans and so skilfully combined the naval and military manœuvres that after six anxious days waiting on the Dutch coast he landed 10,000 of his 12,000 men on the 27th of August, 1799. His dispositions were so brilliant that when at last the French and Dutch attacked him with more than double his numbers, he threw them back with heavy losses of more than 2,000 casualties. The two actions carried through by the Scots commander were so boldly fought that the primary object of the venture was achieved, for all that remained of the Dutch fleet was securely captured. In the meantime more British and Russian troops arrived, and in due course the Duke of York crossed the Channel to take full command. Even then the courage and dash of Sir Ralph could not be eclipsed. The decisive—or rather the indecisive—battle of the 2nd of October brought fresh credit to him, for although it was a drawn battle, he proved his dash and spirit by leading his men onward against the foe, even although two horses were shot under him. Secretary Dundas wrote to young Abercromby on the 6th of September as follows :—" Thanks, however, to Heaven and to Sir Ralph, we stand on a pinnacle of glory and of fame." When an armistice was signed on the 20th of October, 1799, which allowed the British forces to withdraw from Holland, Abercromby was not a little relieved. He returned to find himself the hero of the hour. Parliament offered him its profuse thanks, and the City of London, ever anxious to outdo Parliament, presented the brilliant Scots commander with a golden sword. But Dundas was not to be outdone. He planned a peerage for Britain's greatest soldier, and the Duke of York cordially agreed and suggested the title of Lord Egmont, the scene of Sir Ralph's finest action. The Scot's reaction was characteristic :—" Allow us to go on in the paths of industry in our different pursuits." He did not want a title. Fulsome flattery went further than even a peerage. The king suggested giving a grant of Carib lands in the West Indies, where the soldier had so recently served. This only enraged the lionised hero :—" I am not a beggar or a covetous person to ask private honours or private grants. Good God, sir, what opinion should I have of myself were I to profit from the crimes and forfeitures of such a set of miscreants as the Caribs ! " And so he quashed that.

All that Sir Ralph wanted was to live happily in his beloved Edinburgh. He got his wish—for a few months. The Scottish winter was scarcely over when in April, 1800, he was summoned to London and loaded with the responsibility of another quixotic adventure. This time he was ordered to sail with all despatch to the Mediterranean and make a swift attack on Genoa. With Minorca as a base and a force of some 20,000, he sailed for Genoa, only to find that Napoleon had " beaten him to it " and by the battle of Marengo had secured the seaport. The project had to be called off. Lord Nelson and Lord Keith were lying at Leghorn with the British Fleet, but though Abercromby consulted with them, there was nothing for it but to return to Minorca.

And now came the most futile of all his expeditions. Pitt, whom Sir Ralph had privately described as " very nearly a great man," was determined to use this large force of men lying idle in the Mediterranean. He conceived the idea that " such a task force " could swoop down on Cadiz and demolish the arsenal there, with little or no risk. Orders were dispatched to Lord Keith and Abercromby to combine in this project. They set off from Gibraltar with 20,000 men in 139 ships, on the 2nd October, 1800. But the whole scheme was bungled. Keith was told that he must be " certain of bringing off the army," and this condition was complicated by his discovering that in a south-west wind there was no safe anchorage for his ships at Cadiz. On summoning the town to surrender they discovered that plague was raging in it. 3,000 men were put into the boats and then recalled to their ships. The general postponed the action ; the admiral would not promise to re-embark the army in such an anchorage. It was a see-saw game between the army and the navy, the perfect example of how *not* to carry out " combined operations." It was not the fault of the two patient Scots : the hasty and ill-timed urgency of the Cabinet was to blame. Sir Ralph called off the mad escapade and returned to Gibraltar. Fortunately, the commanders did not lose their good temper. They were comrades in arms to the last.

The administration of Pitt was not disposed to keep a large and well-trained force at Gibraltar doing nothing. On the 24th of October orders arrived for both Keith and Abercromby to make for Egypt, and expel the French. By the 18th of November, the general had reached Malta. The vague and general terms of his commission permitted him to work out for himself a clear and cogent scheme of conquest, and from his notes to Sir John Moore, his indispensable right hand, we see that he planned to sweep down on Alexandria with all speed. But from November to April, gales rage along the Egyptian coast, and in any case much had to be done to bring his force up to concert-pitch. He improved the method of carrying packs, he vetted the personnel of the bands, he improved the texture of the material for the soldier's trousers. Nothing was too personal or individual to be beneath his solicitude.

Although Napoleon had abandoned his forces in Egypt, he was confident they could hold it against any possible attack. Indeed, they turned out to be double the strength of the British expedition, which was only 15,000 men. Their spirit, too, was excellent and they were well-officered. In blissful ignorance of all this, the bold Scot ordered transports to rendezvous at Marmorice, near Rhodes, where Turkish help was to be waiting for them. Turkish treachery did not belie itself. A couple of hundred old horses was all that was added to his force. But he used the time and place well. He came to a clear understanding with Lord Keith about the navy's duties and he drilled his soldiers daily in moving in and out of the boats.

When on the 23rd of February, 1801, the fleet of 175 ships sailed under a steady breeze, only a confirmed optimist could have smiled on the expedition. The experienced pilots of the coast pronounced the attack as insane. Not a single man aboard knew the terrain of the landing-places. The maps available were ludicrously inaccurate. The only possible landing place, Aboukir Bay, was the enemy's strongest point of defence. Only the element of surprise was left in the hands of Sir Ralph. Even this was wrenched from him, for two officers exploring the beach at Aboukir were captured on the 27th of February, and a French frigate spotted the British

fleet and gave ample warning. Friant, the French commander, was waiting for them with 2,500 men skilfully
placed on the commanding hill. It seemed to him too
foolish for even the British to attempt. Change the
names and we might say it was Gallipoli antedated by a
hundred years.

Sir Ralph made a careful examination of the ground
and the beach and believed the thing could be done.
He ordered the *Mondovi*, a brig, to draw inshore and
act as the centre of attack. Each soldier carried sixty
rounds of ammunition, two spare flints, three days' rations,
canteens of water, camp-kettle, blanket or great-coat.
The Grenadiers carried the colour of each battalion.
Zero hour was 2 in the morning of March 8th, but it was
9 before the whole impressive line of boats was ready to
dash to the beach. What a thrilling sight! With a
resounding cheer the whole line dashed forward to the
landing-places and the French guns from Aboukir Castle
roared out. Sir Ralph commanded it all from a bomb-
vessel close in shore, and every man knew that he was
ready to issue the recall if the attack seemed hopeless.
" In grand order, and almost simultaneously, the first
line of boats reached the shore, and in a twinkling 2,000
men were formed up in line. With fixed bayonets, in many
cases without waiting to load, the regiments were led
straight to their front against the enemy, without a
moment's delay or hesitation, some with charged bayonets
in perfect order, others scrambling up the ascent as best
they could, but all pining to take their revenge for the
losses they had been forced to take in silence." (So Col.
A. la Court.) By nightfall the whole force was ashore, a
magnificent achievement. Of the 15,300 soldiers, only
700 were casualties. Let this be compared to the Gallipoli
expedition, which shewed casualties of fifty per cent.!

Were the French doing nothing all this time? Assuredly no. They launched cavalry charges against the landing forces and opened up their biggest guns on the concentrations of troops. But next day the stolid British soldiers advanced, driving the French before them. Three days later they advanced again. Held up again, Abercromby brought up his bigger guns to equalise the superiority of the French. He was now four miles from Alexandria, and drew up his front of a mile and half, so that one wing rested on the sea and the other on Lake Maadieh. Stores, ammunition, guns and tents were now landed and brought forward for use in the line. A reserve line of foreigners was drawn up. Word came through that Menou, the French commander, had arrived in Alexandria with a large army and was spoiling for a fight. The Scots commander told his men to lie in their blankets with fixed bayonets, ready to attack in the dark. Sure enough, the Frenchman on the night of the 20th March made a feint at the British left, but before morning he brought his 21,000 seasoned veterans swinging against the British right. This was exactly the manœuvre used by General Montgomery at El-Alamein. Round the Castle the battle raged. In stony silence the British soldier waited until he could see the glazed hat of the Frenchman and then opened his furious fire. The impetuous French assault petered out.

Before the British Commander-in-Chief had stepped ashore to establish his headquarters, he had remarked to General Hope, " This is taking the bull by the horns," but now he knew that the bull had still a fight in him. Menou was disappointed but fully determined. He brought up his 1,000 cavalry, which charged through the front British line and sought to cut off the reserves behind. Even the Black Watch in reserve had to wheel about and tackle the French horsemen, until not one returned. So dashing and unexpected was their appearance that Sir Ralph was caught unawares. He had always been short-sighted, and was constantly dependent on his son, General Moore or Kempt, to prime him on the dispositions of all the forces in the field. But at this unfortunate moment Colonel Abercromby was actively engaged at another point of the line, and a dragoon cut at the general with his sabre, which passed through his clothes and only slightly grazed his flesh. Moore says that he "was actually taken by a French dragoon, but a soldier of the 42nd shot the man." So the Scot saved his countryman and rank was swept aside.

But if the commander escaped one peril, another fell thick upon him. He had ever scorned danger when the battle raged, and although he often laid it down that an officer must carefully consider his own life, he himself exposed his person in the most foolhardy fashion. His son scented danger in the height of the fight, and, searching, he found his father in the very centre of the line, just where guns were firing at the enemy. A spent ball had lodged in the thigh of Sir Ralph, but he spurned the idea of resting or retiring. " Many poor fellows are worse wounded than me," he remarked, as he continued to direct the manœuvres. But the wound was deep. It was long ere a surgeon was summoned from the Guards, and he failed to find the ball. No wonder, for it had shot upwards and lodged in the thigh-bone. It was beyond medical skill to remove it. Even so, he refused to leave the field of victory till the last shot was fired. By this time, he was so exhausted that he could no longer ride his horse, and it became clear he must re-embark. While lying on a litter aboard Lord Keith's flagship, the *Foudroyant*, an officer snatched a blanket and placed it beneath his head to give him greater ease. He enquired what the object was, and was told, " Only a soldier's blanket." Reprovingly Sir Ralph rejoined, " Only a soldier's blanket! A soldier's blanket is of great consequence, and you must send me the name of the soldier to whom it belongs, that it may be returned to him." Here, indeed, is the thought of the typically great commander. Nor can we forget that the soldier thought equally of his commander, for it is recorded that on the first night of the landing, the 8th of March, 1801, the common soldiers made a comfortable hut of date-palm leaves in which to shelter their chief from the cold night air.

Every care was taken of Sir Ralph. His fever seemed to leave him on the 24th, but the wound must have mortified, for his temperature rose suddenly and the pain was assuaged only by heavy doses of opium. A soldier of sixty-six, bearing the full weight of a decisive and bloody battle, and enduring the full rigours of the field, cannot sustain septicaemia indefinitely, and by the 28th his resistance was virtually ended and he slept away at 11 p.m. without pain or struggle. He had crowned his career with the greatest of all his victories and had turned the tide in the life-and-death struggle with the all-conquering Napoleon. Like Nelson himself, his hour of death was his hour of glory.

His body was taken to Malta and buried with full military honours.

The House of Commons in gratitude commissioned a monument in St. Paul's for Britain's outstanding soldier, and granted a pension to his widow and two succeeding heirs of £2,000 a year, while the king created her Baroness Abercromby of Tullibody and Aboukir.

Not to be outdone, Edinburgh Town Council erected

a monument to him on the wall of the High Church, and staged in his honour a great military display in the Meadows on the 2nd of June.

But how did his victorious army feel? Moore, as soon as he heard the news the very next morning, wrote in his meticulous Diary :—" His death at this period is most unfortunate for his country; but he could have fallen at no moment and under no circumstances more fortunate for his fame. He has conducted the only part of the expedition which is likely to be brilliant; and after beating the French in three successive actions, which is more than has been done by any General in this war, he has died of the wounds he has received in battle. Sir Ralph was a truly upright, honourable, judicious man; his great sagacity . . . made him an excellent officer. The disadvantage he laboured under was being so extremely short-sighted . . . It was impossible, knowing him as I did, not to have the greatest respect and friendship for him; he had ever treated me with marked kindness. The only consolation I feel is, that his death has been that he himself wished, that his country, grateful to his memory, will hand down his name to posterity with the admiration it deserves." Nor was Sir John Moore less frank in his letter home to Britain : " He will be honoured and lamented by his country, and his name handed down to posterity with the most distinguished of his countrymen. This is the consolation I derive from the loss of the best man and best soldier, who has appeared amongst us this war."

Not least in the little village of Tullibody did the blow come home with mingled pride and sorrow. When the classical monument was unveiled in the little parish church, many of those villagers crowding round could recall how the Laird had often graced them with his presence and gladdened their hearts by a kindly word.

Has Time dealt kindly with so pure and grave a heart as that of Sir Ralph ? One feels he is due a fresh wreath, for the world hurries on and men's memories are very short. Under stress of national emotion fulsome words have often been used of national heroes, but the terms of the Order of the Duke of York on the victory of Aboukir were wise and true :—

" The illustrious example of their commander cannot fail to have made an indelible impression on the gallant troops at whose head, crowned with victory and glory, he terminated his honourable career ; and his Majesty trusts that a due contemplation of the talents and virtues which he uniformly displayed in the course of his valuable life, will for ever endear the memory of Sir Ralph Abercromby to the British Army . . .

" His steady observance of discipline, his everwatchful attention to the health and wants of his troops, the persevering and unconquerable spirit which marked his military career, the splendour of his actions in the field, and the heroism of his death, are worthy of the imitation of all who desire, like him, a life of honour and a death of glory."

One might go on long enough adding tribute to tribute, and the lines of glittering generalities would lengthen. Better to pierce to the heart of Abercromby and see two strangely contrasting men. One is the friendly and benevolent country laird, the man of books, the sedate elder of the Kirk, the rustic moralist and the benign philosopher who looks for law and justice to rule the world. Happy in the goodwill of his village acquaintances, he is happier still with his devoted wife and growing family, for his home is the dwelling-place of peace and tranquility. Here, indeed, is the man of peace.

G

In the same heart, however, was the smouldering passion of the fighter. The kindly laird, at the scent of battle, becomes in a trice the eager and agitated man of action. His blood runs high for adventure. He forgets danger. He foresees the moves of his enemy and has his counter-move ready. He thinks ahead with an uncanny instinct for the possible snags. In those combined operations with the British Navy, of which he was the superb pioneer, he revealed at St. Lucia, at the Helder and at Aboukir, an almost miraculous gift for dovetailed organisation. Nor was the plan a mere bloodless scheme ; it was a series of tactful and unruffled personal contacts that swept soldiers and sailors alike into the great enterprise. As he effected each landing on a hostile shore, he became more expert. When he trained his men in boat-drill every day at Marmorice, he never dreamed that he was taking the first step towards D-Day in 1944 and towards an even greater victory than Aboukir.

Sir Ralph was fated to be for ever fighting against heavy odds. The dice seemed loaded against him. The army was a poor, dispirited force before him, and he was supremely the direct personal influence that infused discipline and the fighting spirit into it. Even so, he had to match these battalions always against greater battalions. He was, in action after action, continually outnumbered, and his tasks bordered on the superhuman. Wellington advised a subaltern in the Peninsular War to score the word " impossible " from his dictionary. Abercromby had done this before him. Only his own dash and spirit, backed by the splendid discipline of his men, secured his triumphs or mitigated his defeats. But he was not all dash and devil-may-care. He could, as at Cadiz, resign the chance of spectacular blows in face of foolhardy risks.

Perhaps it was the almost hopeless nature of his successive tasks that forced him to consider so carefully the needs of the common soldier. He cared for his body, with special uniforms and equipment. He cared for his mind, so that instead of being " browned off " with slackness and indifference, the soldier saw his interest in a greater keenness and a stout fighting spirit. This is all the more remarkable, because all Sir Ralph's campaigns were fought by a man who might be thought to have done with life. Instead he shewed a lively vigour, and a dogged bravery that amazed younger commanders. But, surely, the gravest defect of all in a general must be the lack of keen sight ? Even this weakness of short sight he overcame by a skilful choice of subordinates, who acted as his own eyes and stood by him on every field of battle. John Moore, who like his chief was destined to fall on the field of battle, was his constant lieutenant in fight after fight, proving to be not only his eyes, but also his hands and his feet.

Thus on personal and historical grounds, Sir Ralph Abercromby was the foremost of all British generals at the date of his death. He gave new heart to this island people in its lone fight against the mighty European dictator. He had shaggy eye-brows and a strong face, and some thought he suggested a very good-natured lion. If he did not have the histrionic virtues of Horatio Nelson, each of his actions sent a thrill of pride throughout the land, and from the royal bedchamber to the little Scots but-and-ben hopes rose again that freedom would revive in Europe.

Sir Ralph died without knowing that his triumph had decided the fate of Egypt and with it that of Europe. But it had. And his son, writing in 1861, is more prophetic than he dreamed when he suggested :—

" The importance of this service is now understood, and is appreciated by the rapid communication through Egypt which is maintained between England and her possessions in the East; and, if the day should ever arrive, as arrive it may, when Egypt shall again become the battlefield, there is no reason to doubt that the interest and honour of the country will be maintained with equal skill and valour, and crowned with equal success."

To which Bernard Montgomery can say, " Quite; there is no reason to doubt it."

BIBLIOGRAPHY

JAMES ABERCROMBY, LORD DUNFERMLINE—
   Memoir of his father : Sir Ralph Abercromby.   1861.

H. SPENSER WILKINSON, *ed.*—
   From Cromwell to Wellington : twelve soldiers.   1899.   " Abercromby (1734-1801)," by Colonel A. la Court.

Sir JOHN MOORE—
   The diary of Sir John Moore.   Ed. J. F. Maurice.   1904.

CHAPTER IV

SIR JAMES WYLIE

Friend and Physician of Three Czars

THE Scots lad o' parts has always stirred the imagination
of his fellows as a proof that the nation is uncommonly gifted. The inference might be, not that genius
lies obscured among the common people, but that if a
boy from a poor home can shine so brilliantly, how brilliant
must be the nation as a whole. It is indeed true that
boys from humble homes have come to fill the highest
and most responsible posts in the public life of Scotland,
but what is even more romantic—such youths have often
shaped the future of many a foreign country.

The case in point is James Wylie.

He was born in 1768 at the sea-port of Kincardine-
on-Forth in the parish of Tulliallan. His father was
William Wylie and his mother Janet Meiklejohn. We
know little more about them, except that they were plain,
working folks with sons both older and younger than
James. A legitimate inference is that Janet like many
another Scots mother cherished the noble desire to see
at least one of her sons rise to the university status.

Of Kincardine at that time we know something.
The First Statistical Account describes it as a thriving
sea-port. In 1786 no less than 91 ships were registered
as belonging to the port and these amounted in tonnage
to the remarkable figure of 5,461, which exceeded the
neighbouring port of Alloa. Nine ships, including sloops
and brigantines of 300 tons, were on the stocks at the one

time.   The vessels of the port ranged far and wide, some trading in the West Indies and others fishing in the waters of Greenland.   More than 300 sailors manned these ships, carrying coal and barley to Holland and the Baltic and returning with wood, iron, flax and linseed.   In addition to this continental trade, an active business was done in fishing at Kincardine, for 100 cruives or hedges of stakes on the sea-shore aided in securing herring, haddocks and even salmon.

It is seen that a boy of some spirit, reared in the Kincardine of that period, was early aware of the lure of the sea and the passion for foreign travel.

In the eighteenth century the training to be a doctor was a sketchy affair compared to the elaborate medical course of to-day.   It started with an apprenticeship to a general practitioner—a very excellent idea—and only in the later stages did the embryo medico proceed to college.   James Wylie, we understand, was by this custom attached to the local doctor in the village and there began to learn the art and some of the science of medicine.   Even so, the call of the sea was so insistent that he ran off during his training on a convenient ship. If James was indifferent to his career his mother was not. She pursued him, we are told, with maternal determination and brought him back to his studies.

He proceeded in due time to Edinburgh University in order to complete his course.   Lyall, in his *Travels in Russia*, asserts that Wylie graduated there, but this is not borne out by the University records, which state that he matriculated there in 1786, 1787, 1788 and 1789, but did not graduate.   And this is confirmed by the fact that when later he sought to enter the Russian Army he was obliged to pass an examination in medicine (*Lancet*, 7th Aug., 1897).

Why did he not graduate?

One local tradition states that Wylie was implicated in a youthful adventure of sheep-stealing—a serious offence in those days—and going into hiding, he at last escaped only by getting away under a load of hay and later pushing off to sea. Well he knew the severity of punishment for this offence, for not many years before Robert Livingston, a chapman of Crook of Devon, had been sentenced to " be stripped naked of his clothes, and scourged by the hand of the hangman through the whole town of Clackmannan with one of the sheep's head and the four feet hanging about his neck, and thereafter to be banished out of the said shire, with certification that if ever he be found therein after this day and date he shall be proceeded against with the rigour of the law . . . he shall be guilty of death." (*Sheriffdom of Clackmannan*, pp. 74-5.)

Here was penalty enough to drive any offender as far as he could get. It appears to have driven Wylie to Russia.

Other factors, however, may have operated in the mind of the young medico. Up to the seventeenth century all men of medicine in Russia were priests. It was Peter the Great who decided to break this monopoly, and he did it by inviting Scots doctors to go out to Russia. His own personal physician was the interesting Dr. Robert Erskine of Alva, who in the first years of the eighteenth century accompanied Peter on his European tour and enjoyed his intimate friendship. He was followed by a constant stream of adventurous medical graduates from Scottish universities, who sought fortune and fame in a new field of work.

When Wylie arrived in Russia he found quite a colony of Scots doctors. Robert Simpson had joined

Admiral Greig's Fleet in 1774 and by 1792 had risen to
be Chief Surgeon to the Naval Hospital at Kronstadt.
Charles Brown, a graduate of Aberdeen, was accepted into
the Russian medical profession in 1784. Dr. Rogerson,
a native of Dumfriesshire, was the doyen of the medicos,
for he had arrived in Russia in 1766 and lived there for
fifty years. Wylie may have found himself in a strange
land, but they were not all strangers.

As we have seen, the young Scot of twenty-two
summers passed his examination into the Russian army
and was appointed to the Eletsky Regiment. He soon
rose to senior rank and came closely into touch with
Colonel Fenshawe, another soldier of fortune, and as men
of academic education were exceedingly scarce Fenshawe
persuaded Wylie to tutor one of his sons. His next move
was into Moscow and later, we are told, he stayed with a
noble Russian family in the country for a certain time.

During these early years in a new country, the shrewd
Scot devoted much time to extra studies. He applied
himself to medical research, almost entirely without
outside help. Books on medicine were hard to come by,
and as for works in Russian these were almost non-
existent. In 1770 there were only three volumes on
medicine written in that language (*British and Foreign
Med. Review*, volume ii, page 606). He applied himself,
nevertheless, to the study of Russian and was able to write
in this difficult language a treatise on yellow fever. Perhaps
it was this which secured his higher degree, but certain
it is that on the 22nd of December, 1794, King's College,
Aberdeen, conferred on him the degree of Doctor of
Medicine. The college register makes it clear that Wylie
of Russia is referred to, but by an accidental or intentional
confusion the name appears as John Wylie and not James
Wylie. Such an academic honour enhanced his pro-

fessional prestige and improved his own efficiency in medicine.

He was ready now for further promotion and it came through a brother Scot. Dr. Rogerson, already mentioned, was in close touch with court circles, and admiring his application and his capacity for work, he recommended Wylie as operator at the imperial court. It will be understood, of course, that operating was a much more primitive and restricted technique than it is to-day. In typical Russian style, the new doctor, being a bachelor, attached himself to the household of Count Strogonof.

He brought to his new post a host of promising talents. His ability was of an uncommonly high order and it was increasing through widening opportunities. His knowledge of his own science was greater than most of his medical friends, and he excelled them in sheer drive of personality and in his wit and penetration. He was rapidly acquiring the art of handling not only human disease but human beings. These and other rare qualities equipped Wylie to grasp the golden chance, and now the chance occurred.

The emperor of Russia was Paul, and his rule of four and a half years from 1796 to 1801 has been described as "the reign of a madman." His omnipotence "drove him below the line of insanity." It was natural enough that a strong-minded courtier should control or use such a monarch, and Kutaisof, his valet, was just such a man. He gained such an ascendancy over the mind of Paul that he was raised to the rank of a count, and soon acquired both money and large estates. In 1798 this favourite of the Czar developed an inflamed condition on the fore part of the neck, which culminated in a large abscess. This caused not only intense pain but endangered his breathing to the point of suffocation. The court surgeons hesitated to take any action to relieve this unusual condition, and, driven to desperation in the middle of the night, Kutaisof summoned the Scots doctor to his aid. Wylie immediately lanced the tumour, evacuated the pus and afforded instant relief to the patient. The pressure on the trachea was at once relaxed and normal breathing was restored. Next morning the excitable Paul was delighted and surprised to learn the good news and in typical fashion he promptly appointed Wylie to be physician to the imperial court.

This was indeed the psychological moment for the Scot. He at once stepped into the limelight. A witty fellow about the court made the caustic comment that Wylie had made his fortune by cutting Kutaisof's throat, but so far was he from denying it that at his morning levee he repeated the joke to his friends with unfailing regularity. The croakers soon found that Wylie's other name was still wily! The lad from Kincardine was turning out to be not only forceful but exceedingly shrewd. He was quickly taking the measure of his jealous rivals.

Nor was this kind of incident isolated. Time and again he seized difficult and baffling cases with skill, firmness and decision, and so built up steadily a reputation as a good surgeon and an expert lithotomist. True, with such an unstable person as Paul to deal with, he was driven at times to unscientific procedure. The Czar at one time was demanding relief from a constant buzzing in his brain, so Wylie by sleight of hand introduced and then released a buzzing bee from his ear, at which Paul declared himself completely cured. It was this, perhaps, that made Lyall feel Wylie's success to be suspect. Such conduct was excused by the sheer insanity of the monarch. Normally, the Scot was a sound scientist and a shrewd and skilful doctor. At any rate, he was now quite indispensable to the Czar. He accompanied him on his journeys to Moscow and Kazan.

In 1800 he sponsored the erection of the Medico-Chirurgical Academy in St. Petersburg, a first step towards his ambitious scheme for the complete re-organisation of medicine in Russia. It is all the more creditable since the Emperor's mind was steadily deteriorating at this time and he was turning brutally reactionary. For Paul the bell was ready to toll. On the night of the 11th of March, 1801—not the 24th as some stated—a group of discharged and disgruntled officers in a drunken orgy burst into the royal bedroom, strangled the Czar and trampled him to death. Joyneville states that the body of Paul was handed over to three Scots surgeons to dissect. These were Doctors Green, Guthrie and Wylie. So there must have been, as we have suggested, quite a little colony of Scots medical men in Russia. It was to the Kincardine man, however, that the task was given to embalm the mangled remains of the Czar. This task, distasteful enough in all conscience, was in those days considered the function of the doctor. What perplexes us to-day, however, is how Wylie could bring himself to sign a certificate that Paul died from the effects of apoplexy. Joyneville soft-pedals the inference by stating that Wylie must have concluded from the state of Paul's brain that he *would* be subject to apoplexy! The world knew it was simple assassination, and learned of the medical certificate with a smile!

So great was the prestige of the Scot, however, that Alexander, the new Czar, promptly re-appointed him to his influential position at court and before the end of 1801 had made him Body-Surgeon and Physician. Emperors might change, but Wylie moved steadily forward to power, and this power enabled him by 1804 to raise the

St. Petersburg and the Moscow Academies of Medicine
to the full status of training colleges. For thirty years
he retained the high position of President of the Moscow
Academy, and when he died the St. Petersburg Academy
erected a statue to his memory. In 1805 he published
in Russian his contribution to the science of medicine in
the form of a treatise on " The American Yellow Fever."
So broad was he now in his professional views that he could
look with some sympathy on the homœopathic practices
of Hahnemann, much to the horror of his more orthodox
colleagues.

But it was not all red-tape administration for James
Wylie. He could add the human touch when occasion
called.

About this period Russia became estranged from
Britain through the wooing diplomacy of Napoleon, and
several British ships were seized in American waters.
One of these was the " Ann Spittal " of Kincardine, and
the captain, Robert Spittal, and his crew were captured
and thrown into a Russian prison. One of the crew was
John Wilcox, whose mother lived alone at St. Ninians,
near Stirling. But Betty Wilcox, like Janet Meiklejohn,
was " no trembler in the world's storm-troubled sphere."
No sooner did she hear the grim news of her son's fate
than she fetched her stoutest shoes and set off along the
turnpike road to Glasgow and on to Paisley, where she
procured the best available yarn. With this she knitted
the most elaborate pair of socks she could devise, incor-
porating triumphantly the pattern of " The Walls of Troy,"
for the socks were designed for no less a personage than the
Czar of All the Russias. Being herself unable to write,
Betty called in the local schoolmaster of St. Ninians, and
dictated for his writing a suitable letter to the Emperor,
appealing for his clemency in regard to John.

This, however, was but half the battle. How was she to get the letter to Alexander? Fortune now favoured her, for she made contact with a sea-captain of Kincardine, who promised to place the gift and letter in the hands of Dr. James Wylie, and *he* would see it safely into the Czar's hands. The plan worked. Wylie duly pressed the claims of Betty Wilcox, and more quickly than she could ever have hoped young John arrived home a free man, and with him a generous gift of money. But money was too impersonal for Betty. She called in the local clock-maker and instructed him to make a suitably impressive grandfather clock, on which were to be painted these explanatory lines of poetry :—

> " Wha would ha'e thocht it,
> Stockings would ha'e bocht it ? "

This unique time-piece for many a day graced Betty's house in Stirling, and now appears to be located in Newcastle. The incident reflects credit on all concerned, and not least on the kindly influence of the doctor from Kincardine.

Nor was this the only gift that the Czar sent to Scotland. A few years ago it was my privilege to handle in the house of Miss Wylie of Kincardine a beautiful china tea-set, which the Czar had presented to the mother of Sir James Wylie. It was but a slight measure of the debt that Alexander felt for the gifts and friendship of his personal physician.

The rising tide of war in Europe under the mounting ambition of Napoleon caused Russia to look to its military efficiency, and in 1806 Alexander promoted his personal surgeon to be the Inspector-General of the Army Board of Health. This gave him fresh tasks against the day when France and Russia would be at war. His first problem was the complete re-organisation of the medical supplies. He was not a day too soon. Napoleon, like

Hitler after him, made his disastrous decision to invade
Russia. In 1812 the bloody battle of Borodina was fought
in order to save Moscow. It cost both sides 60,000 in
slain and wounded. It was now that James Wylie showed
his mettle. He was no fawning courtier. On the contrary,
he was right on the field of action. There in the heat of
battle he himself performed no fewer than 200 operations,
in a herculean effort to save the wounded and dying.
Although Napoleon was the nominal victor in the fight,
the Cossacks on the night following penetrated far into
the French lines and bivouacked there. Nor was Wylie
a yard behind them on his errand of mercy. Joyneville
(Vol. ii, p. 193) states that the wild Cossacks compelled the
Imperial Guard of Napoleon even after their victory to
stand to arms. When Wylie later met Sir Archibald
Alison in Paris, he assured him that he was present with
the Cossacks on that epic night. There was no lack of
spirit about Wylie.

The Scot took his medical duties very seriously
and, free from the cares of family life, he devoted himself
utterly to Alexander. In November, when the Czar
decided to see war at first hand, he accompanied him to
Vilna and shared with him the unforgettable misery and
carnage of the field. The broken remnants of the Grand
Army, it will be remembered, fell back on Vilna hoping
to enjoy rest and food, but though they " wept for joy at
the sight of a loaf of bread " they had hardly time to digest
it when Platoff and his remorseless Cossacks swept upon
them again and cut many of them down in cold blood in
the streets of the city. The Polish Jews of Lithuania,
forgetting their promises in the exultation of revenge,
joined in the terrible slaughter. It is said that a waggon
of coins was upset across the street and Frenchmen and
Russians, ignoring their feud, engaged in a friendly scramble

for the spoil. But the carnage and the struggle was unforgettable. Neither Czar nor doctor could ever blot it out of memory.

But by next year Buonaparte had recovered from his enormous losses and faced Russia and Prussia with an army of 200,000 men. He forced the Allies back on Leipzic on to Dresden and across the Elbe. It was at Dresden that Alexander had a conference with Moreau, his commander, not far from the scene of action. A cannon-shot struck Moreau and shattered his leg. Wylie, in immediate attendance, examined the limb and decided that amputation was necessary in order to save the life of the general. This was done and it is generally recognised that this alone saved Moreau's life. Lockhart has a slightly different version of the incident, in which both limbs are shattered and Moreau is smoking a cigar while his limbs were being amputated. Though he died some time afterwards, his death was not accelerated by Wylie, who indeed emerges with credit from the incident.

So the campaign moved to its end. Like Hitler in Berlin, so Napoleon in Paris was hemmed in to Paris and his enemies from both sides trampled the streets of his capital. On the 30th March, 1814, Platoff and his Cossacks poured into Paris and bivouacked on the Champs Elysees. The Emperor Alexander with Wylie occupied the most fashionable hotel and prepared to discuss terms with Talleyrand, the wily plenipotentiary of Napoleon. In April Sir Archibald Alison arrived with the British delegation and made contact with the Russians. Here is his word picture :—

"The extreme kindness shown to us by the Russian generals and officers during our stay in Paris led to our giving them a dinner, which was furnished in handsome style at the Restaurant Mapinot in the

Rue St. Honore. Sixteen sat down to dinner and the utmost cordiality prevailed. Count Platoff, General Chernichoff, General Barclay de Tolly, Sir James Wylie, Sir William Crichton and many others honoured us with their presence, and, contrary to the usual practice, the conviviality was prolonged to a late hour. We then saw what was deeply interesting, Russian bonhomie and abandon; and their manners and usages impressed us with a strong sense of their wealth of feeling and sincerity of disposition. As the evening advanced and the *ponche à la Romaine* and iced champagne began to produce their wonted effects, they became, without being noisy or violent, in the highest degree demonstrative in their exuberance. Everyone drank wine with his neighbour after the Continental fashion, touching their glasses before they put them to their lips, and many were the toasts drunk to the ' Eternal Alliance of Great Britain and Russia.' Before parting, the company embraced after the German fashion; and the last thing I recollect is seeing my brother, a man six feet high, lifted up by Platoff, who was six inches taller *and being kissed in the air*." (*Autobiography*, Volume i, page 93.)

Alison found a ready welcome among the Russian officials in Paris, one reason being that he had introductions to the key people (1.77), including Lord Cathcart, the British Ambassador, and this reveals an unexpected and romantic link, for Cathcart's home and estate at Schawpark was situated at a short distance from Wylie's home at Kincardine-on-Forth. After referring to the Scots doctor, Alison continues :—

" The dignified air and courteous manners of the Emperor Alexander, the simple character and

SIR JAMES WYLIE.

unaffected bonhomie of Platoff, the austere look
and weighty observations of Barclay de Tolly, the
joyous habits and youthful enthusiasm of Blucher,
the mingled chivalry and courtesy of Chernichoff,
awakened our respect and admiration and produced
an interest in their achievements, which will never
be effaced . . ."

Alexander, being so near to England, could not
miss the chance of crossing the Channel, and so we find
him, with Wylie, his faithful medical attendant, on the 10th
of June at Hampton Court. Later they attended the
famous Ascot Races, as one of the sights of England, and
it is stated that at the request of the Czar, James Wylie
was knighted on Ascot Heath. The king was hopelessly
insane by this time, and the Prince Regent deputised
for him. With political and poetic justice, he used the
sword of Platoff for the ceremony. Nor was this all.
Before Alexander sailed from Portsmouth on the 2nd
July, he saw Wylie kneel once again—this time aboard a
British Man o' War, to receive the higher dignity of a
baronetcy.

Amid all these functions did Sir James find time
to drive north to Kincardine to see his proud mother?
We do not know, but it is more than likely. One thing
he did do illustrates the shrewdness of his Scots nature.
He planned some day to return to his native soil after his
long exile and " linger out life's taper to a close," and
against that day he made ample provision. He invested
no less than £60,000 in British Funds. As it turned
out, he never did return to his native soil, nor so far as
we know did he marry or have offspring to inherit his
estate. But the move was a palpably wise one. His
relatives down to the present day have cause to thank
him for this far-sighted provision, for after his death and

H

consequent litigation they were destined to enjoy a modest allowance from these funds.

At this point in our romantic story there is a gap of eight years, and in order to fill out the picture of Wylie's life in Russia it is worth giving Lyall's impressions, which, although biased and scant of praise, are nevertheless interesting :—

" Sir James Wylie was reckoned a good surgeon and was well-known as an expert and successful lithotomist before his appointment as operator at court and had acquired much reputation both at Moscow and Petersburgh (sic). Since his appointment to the head of a military department he has been most assiduous in his duties and has much merit for having raised the medical character, introduced numerous improvements into surgical practice and re-organised the military hospitals. With the assistance of a number of professors, he also composed a pharmacopoeia, which has had its use in that empire, though a work of little ingenuity or merit, and unfortunately the knight in his ardour for new names has composed some almost the width of a page, than which nothing could be more ridiculous. A letter of mine, written by his desire, addressed to him and published in the Edinburgh Medical and Surgical Journal nearly nine years ago, points out the folly and the danger of a continual change in pharmaceutical nomenclature.

" In consequence of the favour in which Sir J. Wylie is held, or is supposed to be held, by the Emperor, he has acquired much importance in affairs which do not belong to his department. Princes, generals and officers of all ranks are daily seen at his levees, some of which he treats in the most extraordinary manner, as if they were quite his dependants. But as he has obtained a character for oddity and drollery, whether real or affected, I shall not presume to determine, every liberty is excused. The protection of the Emperor, besides, is a shield against all complaints in a country where the degradation of despotism and slavery is still manifest in all ranks of society, at least to those who have had opportunities of witnessing their transactions when under no restraint.

"Sir James Wylie has avoided private practice. He lives in his apartments in the Imperial Palace in the most economical, I might say niggardly, manner, and seldom or never pays for a dinner. If obliged to remain at home, I have been told that soldier-like he makes his repast of black bread and salt. But, in general, he goes without invitation to some acquaintance either in the Palace or in the city and dines *en famille*, agreeably to the custom of the country. He has acquired considerable wealth, and has now the revenues of two ' arends ' or estates, which the Emperor has bestowed upon him, but he is by no means so rich as many imagine." (R. Lyall, *Travels in Russia* (1825), Volume ii, p. 466 ff.)

The traveller here is clearly seeing Wylie through the distorted lens of jealous courtiers and contemporary medicos in Russia. Yet making due allowance for this, Sir James appears a very amusing and interesting figure in Russian court circles of that age. Certainly, if the canny Scot could leave £60,000 in Britain in 1814 without undue personal inconvenience, he must have been a very rich man by 1824. It is plain from Lyall, too, that he had to calculate all the time on the denigrating gossip of jealous courtiers.

But he more than held his own. The years only strengthened his hold on the idealistic and doctrinaire Alexander, who after the fall of Napoleon determined to set Europe on the way to a lasting peace. The Congress of Verona was convened in 1822 in order that the powers might reach an understanding. The Russian Emperor was to find that the Duke of Wellington, with some of the old iron in his nature, was taking his own line in the new political manoeuvring of Europe, even though this meant departing from the policies of Russia, Prussia, Austria and France. Oblivious to his own pro-Russian policy, Alexander claimed that of all the great powers he alone was unselfish in his aims. Little was achieved by the Congress of Verona, and at the last meeting the Emperor, a depressed and disillusioned man, broke off the conversations, shook hands and walked away. The fact was that he was a victim of nervous debility and was deep in the quagmire of emotional morbidity. This was Wylie's headache, and he was taxed to the limit of his ingenuity to relieve such a condition.

Even when something undeniably painful did touch him, as when bitten in bed by a scorpion, the Emperor was indifferent to Wylie's exertions for his relief. His malady went deeper than a scorpion's bite. It was mental and emotional. To have understood his patient, far less to have cured him, Wylie would have required all the resources of modern psychiatry.

All his life Alexander had longed to see Rome. Perhaps as head of one great Christian Church he had a forgivable desire to meet the head of another. Perhaps the Rome of the mighty Caesars cast its spell upon him. In any case, Wylie seized upon this old nostalgic longing as a welcome diversion for his patient. He proposed they should visit Rome. But at once the neurotic feared other dangers. He might, for instance, be assassinated. Already, even in Verona, he was afraid of stepping outside his hotel, lest in the street the carbonari might shoot at him. Indeed, before he passed down any street he ordered his guards to search it on both sides. Like most neurotics, Alexander covered his hidden fear by a plausible excuse: it would never do for him to visit the Pope lest people thought he was becoming a Roman Catholic. But later Wylie assured Lee categorically that his master was held back from Rome by the fear of assassination. Sir James, it is clear, had not to look for his worries.

Back in Russia, the Emperor failed to recover his good health or his good spirits. Like an inseparable shadow, the Scot followed his master. In January, 1824, they were spending a few days at Czarco-Selo, when a most unfortunate experience befell his imperial majesty. He

"had taken his usual morning walk, often extended to two or three leagues in the park, when he was caught in a heavy shower of snow and rain and received a thorough chill. On his return, he retired to his room, where his dinner was brought to him but he could not touch it, and in the course of the evening was attacked with fever and erysipelas, which appeared on his leg and rapidly spread over his whole body to his head, so that his brain became affected and he was delirious. His attendants removed him in the night in a covered sledge to St. Petersburg, where he was attended by the principal doctors in the capital, and as symptoms of gangrene began to appear they were unanimous, with the exception of Wylie, that it would be necessary to amputate his leg to save his life. This doctor with Scotch caution reflected that if he died under the operation, the Russian nation would be more severe in their criticism than if he perished from the disease, and he took on himself the responsibility of preventing amputation. The doctors were threatened by the mob and were provided with passports in case the illness ended fatally. At last the complaint yielded to cautery and the lancet . . ." (Joyneville, III.341.)

And so events proved Wylie to be right: Even if his line was " when in doubt, do nothing," we must admire the decision and independence of the Scot. This decisiveness in his character was precisely the characteristic required to offset the volatile temperament of the Emperor.

In 1825 Alexander decided to spend some time in the Crimea, and Lee, a doctor who was present on several occasions, was forced to admit that Wylie bore himself worthily. He noted how utterly devoted the Scot was to his master. Through all the campaigns and under the most trying circumstances he behaved in accordance with his high reputation as a man of medicine. Lee, too, records that in this same year, 1825, he watched Alexander and Wylie arrive at the cathedral of Yoursouff accompanied by a few personal attendants. Later, he dined with the royal party, and describes it.

" There were oysters for dinner and a small worm was adhering to the shell of one presented to His Majesty. This was shown to Sir James Wylie, who said it was quite common and harmless, and he reminded the Emperor of a circumstance which had occurred to them at the Congress of Verona in 1822. A person at Verona had then sent to the Emperor to entreat that he would abstain from the use of oysters, as there was a poisonous marine worm or insect in them." (*Last Days of Alexander I*, Volume i, page 26.)

At the same dinner at Yoursouff the conversation turned round to the unorthodox medical ideas of Hahnemann on homœopathy. Count Worouzow asked the royal physician if he would use the homœopathic treatment for inflammation of the brain or bowels or in the fevers of the Crimea, and in particular if a grain of quinine would stop a fit of these fevers. Lee agreed with Wylie that it would.

We now come to the most trying point in the career of Wylie, namely the death of Alexander I. Towards the end of 1825 the Czar, not without warning from his doctor, was engaged in conversation for some time with the captain of a Turkish vessel that had not submitted to the usual precaution of quarantine. Shortly after this incident, the imperial valet, a servant of some twenty-seven years standing, confided in Sir James that his master seemed to him to be ill and pale. Next day on the drive from Diebitch to Mariopol the Emperor experienced a fit of shivering and ague. As the lodging-place that night was uncomfortable, his physician gave him a glass of hot punch and pushed on rapidly to Tagenrog. Not that Alexander was himself apprehensive. On the contrary, he grumbled that his constitution was so stout that he never failed to recover from every ailment. He had the fatalist's indifference to sickness. On this point both Joynville and Schnitzler agree, though the latter admits that the royal patient took some of Wylie's medicine, which relieved his paroxysms of fever and the pains in his head and limbs. But beyond this, he would take no medicine and the desire to live seemed to fail. Sleep, quietness and cold water was all he wanted, but his throbbing head denied him the sleep and Wylie denied him the cold water.

It was time now to take a second opinion, so Dr. Stoffrogen, the physician of the Empress, was called in, and he agreed that leeches would afford some relief. This, however, only enraged His Majesty, who loudly declaimed against the value of all medical skill, and declared himself incurable. Leeches he abhorred—not without cause—as depriving the poor patient of the comfort of praying to his Maker.

The scene was now positively heartrending, for Wylie had to tell the Empress that her husband was gravely ill, but she handed back to him the unwelcome task of breaking the news to Alexander himself. " Then you really think I am dying," replied His Majesty, and pressing the hand of the Scot he added that it was the best news he had heard for years. But the doctor seized his chance and asserted that not to take medicine to avoid death was tantamount to suicide in the eyes of God. The challenge struck home. The Emperor gave in. Later, thirty leeches were fixed on his temples. " Ah, my friend," he assured Wylie, " I think you are deceived as to the nature of my illness ; it is my nerves that need a cure." It was now the end of November and each day saw a change for the worse in Alexander. As the sun broke into his room on the 30th of the month he exclaimed " Ah ! le beau jour ! " Thus he welcomed his last full day. Ere another sun set he was no more.

Schnitzler in his account reveals more of the intimacy and mutual regard that undoubtedly existed between the Czar and his Scots medical adviser. In his extreme condition he drowned with imprecations every suggestion offered by his doctor. " I have no confidence in your potions. My life is in the hands of God ; nothing can stand against His will. Speak to me no more of treatment," shouted His Majesty. He then confessed that his nerves were very much deranged, to which the caustic Scot retorted, " Alas, that is a case more common with sovereigns than with ordinary mortals." " True," confessed the mighty Czar, " and with me in particular there are many reasons why it should be so, and at this moment more than at any other."

Later, when the illness was clearly mortal, he applied to the grave Scot, " They have spoken to me of Holy Communion. In what condition am I really? Am I near my end? " Genuine emotion now overcame the stolid professional physician. Sobs choked his words as he said, " Yes, sire, I now speak not as a physician but as an honest man. It is my duty as a Christian to tell you that you have no time to lose." The Emperor, we are told, seized Wylie's hands and held them long between his own. When the strange, neurotic, idealistic Alexander died at 10.40 a.m. on the 1st of December, 1825, Wylie was standing faithfully by his sofa.

The evidence of Lee at this point is interesting. As a brother-doctor he was actually in close touch with Sir James and he testifies that on November the 27th he went to the residence of Wylie at Tagenrog to get an accurate account of the Czar's condition. There Wylie read to Lee all the daily reports written upon the patient, and Lee was impressed by the scientific explanations offered and by the fact that all the doctors in the court circles concurred in Wylie's diagnosis and treatment.

Lee deals with another point in the case. It had been insinuated—no doubt by detractors of the Scot—that he had mishandled the case of the Czar, especially when he allowed his patient to dictate his professional treatment of him, for he had indeed submitted to his refusal to take medicine. It ran—Why did they not compel His Majesty to submit to their plan of treatment? But the Scot had a very cogent reply, and more cogent in the land of Russia than in his own native Scotland. " In other words," he retorted, " why did they not commit the crime of *lèse-majesté*—a proceeding which no circumstances could ever justify." This was enough for Wylie. To the end he respected the sacred personality of the Emperor.

So one monarch passed away and another came. But, strangely enough, the shrewd Scot remained. It was an exception to the general rule that another Pharoah arose that knew not Joseph. The new emperor, Nicholas, continued to show the royal favour to Sir James, for he was now a kind of institution in St. Petersburg. Indeed, new honours came thick and fast upon him. He was made a Privy Councillor of Russia and his decorations included the orders of St. Vladimir, St. Alexander Nevsky and St. Anne. Foreign honours, likewise, flowed in upon him, such as the Legion of Honour, the Red Eagle of Prussia, the Crowns of Wurtemberg and Leopold of Austria.

Nor could Nicholas even from the start of his reign afford to dispense with his valuable help. In May, 1826, difficulties arose between Turkey and Russia over the Treaty of Bucharest. Russia appears to have dealt brusquely with the " Sick Man of Europe," and demanded ratification at once. Wylie, in charge of Army Medical Services, was ordered to hold himself in readiness. Admiral Greig—another Scot, was warned to prepare the Russian Navy for action. As it turned out, Turkey climbed down and war was averted, if only for another twenty years. Lee comments that Wylie seemed quite disappointed that after all the excitement nothing was to happen. Not indeed that the Scot was a warmonger. On the contrary, he was looking only for the chance to use the organised medical services of the empire, which he had so efficiently built up. Lee, who had made a personal inspection of the Artillery Hospital, gives his verdict that the wards were in excellent order. Against this, we have to place the condition of British military hospitals when thirty years later Florence Nightingale launched her crusade of mercy. In addition to being the first Director of the Academy of Military Medicine, Sir James took hospitalism a stage further by founding the Wylie Clinical Hospital in St. Petersburg.

There is no evidence to show that the great Scot ever lost his grip on the affection and esteem of the Czar's household or lost his prestige as a national figure. If certain croakers were ready to miscall him, he had always skilful and loyal collaborators. The post-mortem examination on the Empress is a case in point. Dr. Lee instances that Wylie gave his report quite objectively and then read to Lee Dr. Stoffregon's report, which coincided completely with it.

A signal proof of his popularity in Russia was given on the occasion of his fortieth year in the service of Russian medicine. This fell in 1840, and is marked by the issue by the Emperor of a special medal, showing on one side the profile of the court physician. In 1897, the medal remained in the possession of a collateral descendant of Wylie, still living in St. Petersburg. (*Lancet*, Aug. 7, 1897.)

So he continued to hold a unique place at court to the last. No denigrating talk ever ousted him from his eminence. It was a place of his own making, the creation of his native character, the result and achievement of his strong personality. In any country, James Wylie would have been outstanding. In Russia he was dominating. He gained power, personal, social and political, and he held it to the end.

The last years of Sir James Wylie were clouded by the threatening clouds of war between Russia and his own native land. Turkey's extreme weakness invited

the marauding instincts of the Czars to plunder a rich
neighbour, and the nephew of Napoleon joined with
Britain to pay off some old scores with Russia. All too
clearly the knowing Scot at the court of St. Petersburg
saw the British anger rising under the lash of Palmerston's
tongue. He saw that soon the fabric of his great military
medical machine would be tested, the task to which he
had given his life's blood. But he did not see it happen.
He passed away on the 2nd of December, 1854, at St.
Petersburg, and on the 27th of the same month Britain
declared war on Russia.

The Czar and all the court notables attended his funeral.
No foreigner ever evoked from the Russians such ample
tokens of grief, nor had any lavished such service upon
them. In life he gave them much ; in death he also gave
them much. He bequeathed to the Czar all his Russian
wealth ; all except £100,000, which he directed should
go to the building of an Army Medical Academy, which
should always be associated with his name.

Nor was gratitude wanting on the part of the Russians.
When the Academy was completed, the centre of the
quadrangle was filled with a striking life-size statue of
Sir James. Carved in grey marble, it showed the great
doctor in a sitting position, holding in one hand the
reformed Statues of the Academy. Caryatides adorned
the angles of the pedestal, and between them were bas-
reliefs, representing incidents from the life of Wylie. To
give special dignity to the whole, the coats-of-arms of
both Wylie and the Academy were added to the panels.

And so Russia honoured the great Scots doctor, who
had spent himself in her service.

It is a fine tale. The boy from the banks of the
Forth rose by sheer grit to sway the lives and fortunes
of the Romanoffs. This is a destiny dazzling enough for

the emulation of aspiring youth, and if the moralist enters his caveat against the lure of imperial power and prestige, we may rejoin that Wylie's was not the greatness that inflicts military defeats with wounds and sufferings, but rather the truer greatness that softens and relieves such woes.

Even among his co-professionals there were those who said that a medical adviser must confine himself to his medicine. Cobbler, stick to your last, was their cry. But Wylie, just by his medical efficiency, was forced into vaster administrative tasks that bordered all too often upon the political, and who shall draw the line precisely between the one and the other? Others thought that his personal influence upon the Czars was too great for a mere man of medicine. No doctor should have his finger so deeply in the domestic and courtly pies of the imperial palace! But it is a doctrinaire criticism. Given emperors like the Romanoffs, unstable, half-crazy, irresponsible, it was a mercy that a man of Wylie's character, wisdom and ability and not a scoundrel like Rasputin guided the head of the vast empire of Russia. What wealth James Wylie derived from the Czars he in the end gave back to them.

Take him, then, for all in all, and you have a strong, shrewd and self-reliant Scotsman. With no adventitious aids, he arrived in a strange land and had to make his career. With only his lancet and his character, he carved his way right into the imperial heart. Portraying the distinctive qualities of his race, he built upon sound professional knowledge a legendary prestige, which cast a spell over the vast millions of Russia for more than a generation.

It is good to revive the memory of such a Scot, and ere it passes, as pass it may, to offer it a generous salute!

BIBLIOGRAPHY

Article on Sir JAMES WYLIE (1768-1854).
Dictionary of National Biography.

ROBERT LEE—
The last days of Alexander I and first days of Nicholas. 1854.

C. JOYNEVILLE—
Life and times of Alexander I. 3 vols. 1875.

J. H. SCHNITZLER—
Secret history of Russia under Alexander and Nicholas. 2 vols. 1847.

Sir ARCHIBALD ALISON—
Some account of my life and writings : an autobiography. 2 vols.
1883.

ROBERT LYALL—
Travels in Russia, the Krimea, the Caucasus, and Georgia. 2 vols.
1825.

The Lancet. 18th March, 1854.

British and Foreign Medical Review, vol. I.

INDEX

I